Too Big to Innovate

How Growth Stifles Disruption in Large Corporations

Souheil Benzerrouk, Ph.D.

DISCLAIMER

This book presents analysis, commentary, and opinion on innovation, corporate culture, and leadership. The companies, case studies, and examples discussed are drawn from publicly available sources, historical records, and the author's professional interpretation.

While care has been taken to ensure factual accuracy, this work does not claim to provide exhaustive or insider accounts of the organizations mentioned. All observations and conclusions reflect the author's perspectives, intended for educational and analytical purposes only.

The inclusion of any company, brand, or individual does not imply endorsement or criticism. Names and examples are used to illustrate ideas about innovation and organizational behavior, not to assign blame or intent. Readers are encouraged to consult diverse sources and form their own conclusions.

In a field as dynamic as innovation, facts evolve. This book aims to capture patterns, not verdicts.

Dedication

To my parents, for their unwavering love, sacrifice, and the values they instilled in me.

To Nadjet, my beloved wife and steadfast partner, your support, patience, and faith give me strength every day.

To Tarek, Hassiba, and Riyadh, you are my greatest inspiration and the reason I strive to be better. May you always dream big and walk your path with purpose.

To my community, thank you for the encouragement, sense of belonging, and shared journey. This work is as much yours as it is mine.

And to my former colleagues, whose thoughtful conversations, debates, and shared experiences helped ignite the ideas behind this book, your insights and camaraderie left a lasting mark.

Table of Contents

Introduction: When Growth Forgets How to Move

Innovation doesn't die in crisis. It dies in comfort. Not with an announcement, but with a meeting.

The decks still glow, the reviews still close, the charts still climb. From the outside, the company looks alive, profitable, disciplined, "well-managed." But inside, something has shifted. The rooms feel heavier. The ideas sound familiar. People start to optimize instead of imagine. Somewhere along the line, growth replaced motion.

No one meant for it to happen. Every process began as protection, a guardrail to reduce risk, a workflow to ensure quality, a gate to keep the bad ideas out. But over time, those guardrails became walls. The system that once produced invention now produces reports about invention. Energy becomes ceremony. Curiosity becomes compliance. The company stops learning faster than the world changes, and that's when decline begins.

The irony is that this happens because of success. Scale was supposed to create leverage; instead, it creates inertia. Process was supposed to protect quality; instead, it protects the past. And leadership, once the spark of vision, becomes an exercise in managing risk rather than expanding possibility.

This book is about what happens when growth turns against its own DNA, when the structures built to make a company reliable make it predictable, and when predictability becomes the enemy of relevance. It's about why large corporations, no matter how visionary their beginnings, lose the instinct to move, and how some rediscover it before it's too late.

The timing could not be more urgent. Artificial intelligence, automation, and global competition have redrawn the map of innovation. What once took quarters now takes weeks. Startups can scale with rented infrastructure. Algorithms can out-analyze strategy departments. Talent can move faster than HR can approve a requisition. The old corporate rhythm, built around annual plans and quarterly earnings, simply can't breathe in an environment that changes by the hour.

The organizations that will survive are those that learn faster than they grow. That requires a new architecture, one that treats innovation not as a project, but as a property of the system itself.

This book follows that path in three acts:

- **Part I: The Systems That Slow Us** how bureaucracy, shareholder pressure, and risk-averse leadership quietly drain a company's creative energy.
- **Part II: The Mechanics of Renewal** the structural and cultural rewiring that makes innovation inevitable, not episodic.
- **Part III: The Future of Motion** how AI, automation, and a new generation of leaders are forcing companies to rebuild their operating systems for speed, learning, and moral clarity.

You will not find motivational slogans here. You'll find mechanics, ways to design for curiosity, for dissent, for learning at scale. Because innovation isn't a department. It's a temperature, and every system either conducts heat or absorbs it.

If you lead a company that has grown successful enough to slow itself down, this book is for you. If you work in one, it's a field guide for remembering how to breathe.

The goal is not to be faster for its own sake, but to build organizations that stay alive in motion, companies that can scale without ossifying, lead without controlling, and keep rediscovering what made them great before they became too big to change.

PART I
Understanding the Growth–Innovation Paradox

Growth begins as a rebellion. A small group of people, armed with little more than an idea and audacity, set out to change something that feels too slow, too broken, too obvious. They build in garages, basements, and borrowed offices. They improvise because they have to. They learn faster than they can afford to fail.

Every great company is born in motion, not because it knows where it's going, but because it refuses to stand still. The founders don't talk about innovation; they live it. Speed is instinct. Risk is currency. Uncertainty is the price of invention.

Then, success arrives. And with it comes something far more dangerous than failure: safety.

The company scales, and with scale comes weight. Process replaces pulse. Planning replaces curiosity. What was once a bet becomes a business model, and what was once a mission becomes maintenance. The same structures that made growth possible begin to harden into walls. The company stops running toward opportunity and starts defending its perimeter.

This is the Growth–Innovation Paradox, the quiet betrayal of progress. The habits that made a company exceptional at starting make it terrible at restarting. Every safeguard becomes a drag coefficient. Every metric meant to measure excellence begins to measure conformity. The system learns to optimize, not imagine.

No one notices at first. The meetings are still full, the charts still climb, the slogans still sing about "disruption" and "transformation." But the spark that once defined the company has been domesticated. The ideas get smaller. The cycles get slower. The passion that once fueled invention is rerouted into self-preservation.

This part of the book is about understanding how that happens, how success calcifies into bureaucracy, how bureaucracy breeds fear, and how fear dresses itself up as discipline. We'll dissect the forces that turn curiosity into caution: the layers of management that multiply, the shareholders who demand predictability, the leaders who mistake control for clarity.

We'll study the quiet physics of corporate decay, how innovation doesn't die by rejection, but by dilution. How meetings stretch time until urgency fades. How the rituals of alignment become the enemies of momentum.

But we'll also look for clues, moments when companies escaped this cycle. When leaders recognized that scale without imagination is slow death. When they learned to trade permission for purpose, hierarchy for trust, compliance for curiosity.

Because the paradox isn't inevitable. It's just unexamined. Growth doesn't have to kill innovation, it only does when we stop asking why we're growing in the first place.

Every company starts with an act of defiance. The question is whether it can keep rebelling against its own success.

Let's begin there, at the moment when freedom turns into formality, and the company that once changed the world forgets how to change itself.

CHAPTER 1

The Growth–Innovation Paradox

The Growth Trap: How Success Turns Against Innovation

Every great company begins as a defiance. Someone, somewhere, refuses to accept the limits of the possible. They see a better way, faster, cheaper, smarter, more humane, and they chase it with unreasonable urgency. In those first fragile years, innovation isn't a function or a department. It's survival. Every risk feels necessary. Every obstacle is personal. These companies start as outsiders with nothing to lose, and that is their greatest advantage. They move before they're ready. They make decisions in hours, not months. They experiment recklessly because standing still would mean extinction. Their cultures are built not on stability, but on motion.

And for a while, motion is enough. Then success arrives. Customers grow. Revenue stabilizes. Investors take notice. What once felt like chaos begins to look like a business. This is the moment every founder dreams of, the point where the idea becomes an institution. But hidden inside that success is the first seed of decline: the shift from *offense to defense.* The startup that once measured itself by how much it could change the world now measures itself by how little it can risk losing. Growth demands systems, but systems demand obedience.

This is the Growth Trap, the paradox that turns every disruptor into the very thing it once sought to disrupt. As companies scale, they build structures to protect what they've achieved, systems of control, predictability, and efficiency. But over time, those same systems choke the freedom, experimentation, and urgency that once made success possible.

At first, those systems work. Processes create consistency. Metrics bring accountability. Policies prevent chaos. Investors reward discipline. The organization begins to look professional, stable, reliable, safe. But beneath that safety, something vital starts to erode: the company's ability to move.

You can see this erosion everywhere. At its peak, Google was the undisputed epicenter of AI. It had the people, the data, and the computing power. But when OpenAI launched ChatGPT, Google hesitated, trapped by its own success. Releasing a raw, experimental model could threaten its reputation, its brand, and its lucrative ad ecosystem. So it waited. And in that hesitation, it lost the very speed that once defined it.

Meta did not lack resources; it lacked courage. After dominating global communication, it tried to engineer another revolution through the metaverse, but built it like a government project: expensive, bloated, and internally fragmented. The result was not invention, but inertia. Netflix, which once reinvented how the world consumes entertainment, now spends its energy defending market share against competitors that learned from its playbook. Boeing, which once embodied the soul of engineering, let financial metrics overpower technical excellence, until the consequences became unthinkable. Even Disney, long a symbol of creative daring, stumbled as its structures multiplied and its decision-making slowed. In each case, the problem wasn't intelligence, talent, or capital. It was gravity, the gravitational pull of growth.

The logic of scale is seductive:

- Systems make things efficient.
- Hierarchies bring order.
- Predictability comforts investors.

But in the pursuit of efficiency, organizations forget that innovation thrives on inefficiency, on mistakes, collisions, and risk. The more a company optimizes for reliability, the more it sterilizes the very conditions that allow discovery.

Growth doesn't just create bureaucracy; it *requires* it. And once bureaucracy takes root, it becomes self-justifying. Soon, the mission shifts from *"build something new"* to *"don't break what's working."*

That's the moment a company begins to die, not publicly, but spiritually.

You can almost plot the progression like a biological cycle:

1. **Rebellion**, A small group breaks the rules and builds something extraordinary.
2. **Repetition**, The company codifies what worked into systems and processes.
3. **Protection**, Those systems become sacred; deviation becomes risk.
4. **Decline**, Innovation slows, creativity fades, and the culture calcifies.

By the time the symptoms are visible slower launches, cautious leaders, disengaged talent, the illness is already systemic.

The Growth Trap doesn't announce itself; it creeps in through success stories, best practices, and five-year plans. It hides in the spreadsheet, in the boardroom, in the meeting agenda. It disguises itself as discipline, professionalism, and control.

And because every large company believes it's immune, nearly every large company eventually falls victim to it.

What's remarkable is that the trap is not inevitable, it's behavioral. Some companies manage to grow without losing their instinct for movement. Microsoft, under Satya Nadella, as we will discuss later dismantled old hierarchies and replaced fear with trust. Moderna proved that a young biotech could act with startup urgency even under global pressure. And Amazon, for much of its life, institutionalized experimentation, embedding agility into its structure rather than fighting against it.

These examples don't disprove the Growth Trap, they reveal how deliberate leadership and cultural design can resist it. The trap is not the byproduct of size alone, but of mindset: when preservation replaces ambition, and control replaces curiosity.

This chapter explores how that transformation unfolds, structurally, culturally, and psychologically. We'll look at how speed hardens into process, how managers replace makers, and how fear of loss quietly becomes stronger than the desire to win.

We'll examine:

- How organizational structures evolve from nimble to bureaucratic.
- Why shareholder pressure reinforces short-term thinking.
- How leadership shifts from visionary to managerial.
- Why internal resistance stops companies from disrupting themselves.

And we'll begin with the most subtle, and dangerous, shift of all: the loss of agility.

The Corporate Structure Problem: How Growth Stifles Agility

In the beginning, structure barely exists. The founders sit five feet from the engineers, who sit ten feet from the customers. The feedback loop is instant. Problems are spotted, debated, and solved in real time. No one needs permission to act because the mission itself is permission.

A new idea can be tested by lunchtime and iterated by dinner. Mistakes are small and frequent, but so are breakthroughs. In this early stage, companies operate less like organizations and more like living organisms, responsive, adaptive, and alive.

This proximity to action is what gives startups their power. They are close to the work, close to the users, and closest to the truth.

The Startup Advantage

Speed, not size, is their strength. When something goes wrong, the same people who built it fix it. When an opportunity appears, they chase it without forming a committee. Hierarchies are irrelevant because trust replaces protocol.

At Medtronic in its early years, engineers and doctors worked shoulder to shoulder, testing prototypes of the first pacemakers in hospital labs. The development cycle wasn't measured in quarters, it was measured in conversations. Each iteration emerged from the friction between invention and necessity.

Decades later, Moderna showed what that kind of integration looks like at scale. During the COVID-19 pandemic, it collapsed the barriers between research, manufacturing, and regulatory affairs. Scientists, engineers, and managers worked as one unit , not a sequence of departments, and what normally takes ten years took less than one.

This is what organizational theorists often miss: innovation is not a function of size or budget, but of *distance*. The shorter the distance between idea and execution, the faster the company learns. The longer that distance becomes, the slower it grows, even when it appears busy.

The Slow Drift Toward Bureaucracy

Growth always begins innocently. At first, new layers of management seem practical. You need people to coordinate projects, standardize quality, manage suppliers, and report progress. You add teams to reduce friction, but each new team adds its own.

The founders who once made decisions in a hallway now sit in boardrooms. The engineers who once stayed late to prototype now stay late to prepare slides. The company still moves, but now it moves *through process*.

No one plans this transition. It happens gradually, almost invisibly. Meetings multiply to improve alignment. Forms appear to increase accountability. Approvals expand to prevent mistakes. Each addition makes sense on its own, but together, they form a maze.

Inside that maze, decisions slow. Creativity fades. And a new hierarchy emerges, one not built on ideas, but on permission.

When Speed Meets Scale

The irony is that these systems work, until they don't. They keep the trains running, but they also make it impossible to build new tracks.

Consider an engineer inside a large company who needs a simple component to test a new design. he submits a request. That request travels upward for approval, to his manager, his department head, and sometimes to finance. Procurement adds vendor reviews. Legal checks contracts. Then logistics adds its delay. By the time the part arrives, the opportunity that inspired it is gone.

The company hasn't just slowed an engineer, it's slowed time itself.

These procedural bottlenecks are the corporate equivalent of entropy: the natural decay of motion into stability. Everyone is working, but few are advancing. The same energy that once built the company now circulates endlessly within it, trapped in loops of compliance and coordination.

When Control Replaces Craft: The GM Example

Few stories capture the quiet transformation from innovation to inertia more vividly than that of General Motors.

In the mid-20th century, GM wasn't just an automaker, it was the heartbeat of American industry. Its cars defined aspiration; its factories defined modern manufacturing. Engineers were heroes, and managers were stewards of progress. The company built more than vehicles, it built an identity of precision, pride, and possibility.

But power, like gravity, has a pull. As GM grew, it began to optimize for control. To manage its vast empire of brands, Chevrolet,

Pontiac, Buick, Oldsmobile, Cadillac, the company created layers of structure so intricate that it soon resembled a government more than a business.

Each division had its own leadership, marketing teams, engineering pipelines, and P&L accountability. On paper, it was a masterpiece of organization, a model of how to manage complexity. In practice, it became a maze.

Decisions that once required a phone call now required consensus. A new design needed sign-off from multiple divisions, budget approvals from finance, and production clearance from procurement. By the time a car reached the assembly line, the market had already moved on.

The tragedy wasn't incompetence; it was alignment. Every division did exactly what its incentives told it to do, protect its turf, hit its quarterly numbers, and avoid mistakes. But when every team optimizes locally, the system fails globally.

By the 1980s, GM's structure had hardened into ritual. Managers spent more time managing *meetings* than managing performance. Product teams designed cars by committee, producing vehicles that were perfectly mediocre, safe, familiar, and uninspired.

Meanwhile, across the Pacific, Toyota and Honda were redefining how a company could build cars. They eliminated silos, flattened hierarchies, and empowered factory workers to stop production lines when something was wrong, an act that would have been unthinkable in Detroit. Toyota's philosophy of *kaizen*, or continuous improvement, wasn't a manufacturing tactic, it was a cultural rebellion against bureaucracy.

GM watched, studied, and documented Toyota's methods in thick binders. But it couldn't implement them, because the problem wasn't in its production process, it was in its organizational DNA. You can't copy agility into a system that rewards caution.

As the years went on, GM's symptoms became familiar: slow product cycles, internal rivalries, and the quiet erosion of craftsmanship. The company still had brilliant engineers, but they were buried under managers. It still had creativity, but it was filtered through layers of review. Every decision needed validation. Every innovation needed permission. And permission takes time, the one resource innovation never has.

When the financial crisis hit in 2008, GM was already hollowed out by its own weight. Its bankruptcy the following year wasn't just the collapse of a balance sheet; it was the collapse of a system that had long outlived its purpose. The structures that once brought discipline had become monuments to themselves.

In the postmortem analyses that followed, few questioned GM's intelligence or intent. What failed was *coordination*. The company could manage anything, except movement.

GM's story is not unique; it's archetypal. It shows how structure, introduced to manage growth, becomes the architecture of stagnation. The problem isn't that complexity exists, it's that complexity becomes sacred. Rules that were meant to ensure quality turn into rituals that block it. Managers, once enablers, become gatekeepers. And a system designed for speed becomes a system designed for safety.

That's the great irony of organizational growth: the same desire to *control success* eventually destroys the capacity to *create it*.

The Hierarchy Dilemma

When Order Becomes the Enemy of Movement

Every growing company eventually faces a quiet reckoning, a moment when the question shifts from *"How do we innovate?"* to *"How do we manage?"* It begins as a practical concern: more people, more products, more coordination. But beneath that practicality lies a subtle transformation, the moment when order stops enabling motion and starts replacing it.

Structure promises clarity, but clarity comes with a cost: the loss of improvisation. And once a company loses its ability to improvise, it loses its instinct to create.

From Collaboration to Control

In a small organization, hierarchy is irrelevant because everyone knows each other's purpose. Titles matter less than proximity, you can turn to your left and find the answer. In a large company, that proximity disappears, so leaders build systems to recreate it. They draw boxes, define roles, and establish chains of approval. It works, at first. But soon, the boxes become walls.

Each new layer of structure promises efficiency while quietly creating distance: distance between thinkers and doers, between decisions and their consequences, between leadership and reality.

The paradox is simple: structure is supposed to make things happen faster, yet every addition makes the organization slower.

The Seduction of Hierarchy

Hierarchy is seductive because it feels safe. It offers clear authority, defined responsibility, and predictable flow. Everyone knows who to ask, who to report to, and what to deliver.

But what begins as guidance becomes governance. And governance, when worshipped, turns into paralysis.

In hierarchical systems, people learn to move only when told. Decisions climb ladders for validation, ideas are polished until they lose their spark, and fear of stepping out of line replaces the thrill of stepping ahead.

By the time a proposal reaches senior leadership, it's no longer bold, it's beige. It has been reviewed, adjusted, and stripped of its risk by committees whose job is to "de-risk innovation," as if such a thing were possible.

Flat Organizations: Freedom at a Cost

In response, many companies try to swing the pendulum the other way. They flatten their structure, remove titles, and preach autonomy. At first, it's exhilarating, decisions speed up, collaboration flows, and people rediscover ownership.

But without structure, freedom can turn to chaos. Responsibilities blur, accountability dissolves, and decisions overlap. A company without hierarchy can ship great ideas, until it has too many of them.

Flat organizations often mistake the absence of structure for creativity. But creativity without direction burns out as fast as bureaucracy kills it.

True agility lies not in having no structure, but in designing one that breathes, one that provides guidance without suffocation.

The Matrix Mirage

To solve the tension between freedom and control, many large corporations adopt the matrix structure, a hybrid system where employees report to two managers: one for their function (say, engineering or marketing) and one for their product or region.

In theory, this design enables collaboration across silos. In practice, it often creates confusion. Employees spend as much time managing relationships as managing outcomes. Priorities conflict, authority overlaps, and progress slows under the weight of alignment.

The matrix was meant to unlock agility; instead, it institutionalized negotiation.

Microsoft, in its pre-Nadella years, was a prime example. Brilliant engineers spent more energy defending their product groups than building great products. Teams competed internally for resources, duplicating work while the company lost ground to faster rivals. The organization wasn't starved of talent, it was starved of coherence.

When Satya Nadella took over, his first act wasn't to reinvent technology, it was to simplify structure. He tore down silos, removed competing hierarchies, and reminded Microsoft that alignment is not a document, it's a shared purpose.

The Laws of Structural Gravity

No matter how it's designed, hierarchical, flat, or matrix, every structure follows the same law: as organizations grow, control gravitates upward. Even well-intentioned leaders find themselves approving what they once empowered. Decisions that used to take a day now take a week. A culture that once rewarded experimentation begins to reward compliance.

Over time, the organization becomes expert at management and amateur at movement. The people who rise are those who protect predictability, not those who challenge it. And slowly, innovation becomes something to schedule rather than something to feel.

The tragedy isn't that structure exists; it's that it becomes sacred. When a process is no longer questioned, it stops serving its purpose.

The Structural Reckoning

Every successful organization eventually reaches this crossroads:

- Add more structure and risk stagnation.
- Remove structure and risk chaos.
- Or learn to live in the tension, building systems that move, not just manage.

The organizations that endure are those that recognize hierarchy as a tool, not an identity. They know when to centralize and when to let go, when to codify and when to break rules. They understand that agility isn't the absence of order, it's the art of designing it lightly enough that people can still breathe.

Because in the end, no structure, however elegant, can save a company that has forgotten how to move.

The Human Cost of Order

How Structure Changes People Before It Destroys Innovation

No system stays mechanical for long. Once structure takes hold, it doesn't just organize work, it reshapes the people inside it. It teaches them new instincts, new fears, new ways to behave.

Bureaucracy is rarely imposed by force; it's absorbed by culture. Over time, people learn what gets rewarded, what gets ignored, and what gets punished. They stop asking what's possible and start asking what's *permitted*.

That's the quiet shift, the moment when innovation ceases to be a mindset and becomes a meeting agenda.

From Builders to Bureaucrats

In the early days, companies are built by *makers*. They are restless, impatient, and emotionally invested. They stay late not because someone told them to, but because they're chasing the high of creation, the electric satisfaction of solving something difficult.

But as organizations mature, the rewards change. Success starts to favor the *managers*, those who can navigate the system, not those who challenge it. The same people who once pushed boundaries now learn to protect them. They still care. But their energy is redirected inward, toward process, compliance, and presentation. They stop building things and start building decks. They stop testing ideas and start testing messaging. And soon, the company is full of professionals, competent, courteous, and quietly disengaged.

The Psychology of Safety

Inside large corporations, risk takes on a moral quality. To take a risk is no longer seen as bold, it's seen as reckless. Caution becomes a virtue. Prudence becomes a form of loyalty.

No one writes this policy down. But everyone feels it. It's there in the way a junior engineer hesitates to challenge a flawed plan. It's there in how a manager edits an ambitious idea until it sounds "more realistic." It's there in the tone of emails that say, *"Let's align before moving forward."*

The organization doesn't have to ban courage; it simply stops rewarding it.

In time, people learn the one rule that governs all bureaucracies: *You will never be fired for following the process.* That lesson spreads faster than any memo.

The Disappearing Voice

Every large company has a point when the most creative voices stop speaking up. Not because they've lost ideas, but because they've lost faith that ideas matter.

They've watched too many meetings end with "Let's revisit this next quarter." They've seen too many prototypes buried under "strategic realignment." They've learned that a quiet career is safer than a bold one.

The innovators don't burn out, they *fade out.* They learn to sound reasonable, to speak the language of consensus. They adapt so well that one day, they look in the mirror and realize they've become the very system they once fought against.

Some leave, to startups, to smaller firms, to anywhere that still feels alive. Others stay, convincing themselves that their caution is wisdom. Both are casualties of order.

The Erosion of Meaning

The most dangerous cost of bureaucracy isn't inefficiency, it's *emptiness*. When people spend years inside systems that measure everything except purpose, they begin to confuse activity with achievement.

Reports replace results. Process replaces progress. Meetings replace movement.

Work becomes performance, a theater of productivity where everyone appears busy but nothing truly changes. Ambition is reduced to compliance, creativity to maintenance.

And when meaning disappears, so does energy. The company doesn't collapse. It just stops caring.

The Subtle Corruption of Talent

In time, even brilliance adapts to bureaucracy. The most intelligent people in the room stop using their intelligence to invent; they use it to *survive*. They learn which phrases calm executives, which metrics sound impressive, which PowerPoint template gets approved fastest.

This is how bureaucracy perpetuates itself, by turning talent into its defender. Those who could fix the system become invested in keeping it stable. And so, generation by generation, the organization gets smarter at explaining its own stagnation.

When Structure Becomes Identity

At a certain point, the system stops being a tool and becomes a culture, even a personality. Ask someone why things are done a certain way, and they'll say, "That's just how we operate." It sounds harmless, but beneath it lies a profound truth: the organization has stopped thinking.

When a company's processes become its identity, change feels like betrayal. Innovation requires self-doubt, but bureaucracy builds self-certainty. It convinces itself that consistency is success, that growth is proof of health.

The greatest danger isn't that people resist change. It's that they no longer believe change is possible.

The Quiet Exit

Every large company loses people long before they quit. They check out mentally, then emotionally, long before they hand in their badge. They still attend meetings, answer emails, and hit their KPIs. But something vital, curiosity, courage, conviction, has already left the building.

This is the invisible attrition of bureaucracy: not of headcount, but of heart. It doesn't show up on an earnings report, but it's the truest indicator of decline.

Because when an organization stops inspiring its people, it has already stopped leading its industry.

The Human Equation of Innovation

Innovation isn't a process, it's an act of belief. It depends on people who still think something better is possible, even when the system tells them otherwise. But belief doesn't survive in a culture of constant control.

That's the human cost of order: the slow replacement of imagination with obedience, of ownership with procedure, of passion with policy.

Every company pays it, but few realize the bill comes due long before the balance sheet shows it.

Conclusion: When Growth Becomes Gravity

Every great company begins with movement, fast, fearless, uncoordinated movement. It grows by saying yes to risk, yes to speed, yes to possibility. But as success compounds, something subtle begins to shift. The company starts saying yes to structure. And then, without noticing, it begins saying no to change.

Growth, once the product of freedom, becomes the force that limits it. What began as a system for progress slowly becomes a system for preservation. Meetings replace motion. Approval replaces initiative. And the organization that once existed to shape the future becomes a machine for protecting the past.

This is the hidden law of corporate evolution: every system eventually serves itself. At first, it serves the mission. Then it serves the process. Finally, it serves its own survival.

The real tragedy isn't that companies slow down, it's that they start believing slowness is wisdom. They confuse caution for strategy and predictability for stability. And by the time they realize the cost, the habit of movement has already been forgotten.

The Growth Trap doesn't destroy companies overnight. It changes them cell by cell, meeting by meeting, until the culture that once created greatness is replaced by one that maintains it. The engineers become managers. The innovators become administrators. The company keeps growing, but inward, not forward.

What began as a story of invention becomes a story of maintenance. And that's when a new force emerges, subtle, silent, and far more dangerous than complexity itself: bureaucracy.

Bureaucracy is what happens when structure becomes ideology, when the rules that once enabled progress become sacred, and no one remembers why they were written. It is the point where management stops managing reality and starts managing itself.

In the next chapter, we'll cross that threshold. We'll see how bureaucracy creeps in, how it multiplies under the banner of professionalism, and how it slowly replaces motion with maintenance, efficiency without energy, order without purpose. Because if growth is gravity, bureaucracy is the atmosphere it creates, dense, invisible, and suffocating to anything that still wants to fly.

CHAPTER 2

The Bureaucracy Trap: How Red Tape Slows Innovation

The Slow Death of Speed

Every great company begins as a story of velocity. It starts in a garage, a borrowed lab, or a cramped office with more passion than process. There is no hierarchy, no permission required, only urgency. Someone has an idea; someone else says *"let's try it."* By nightfall, there is something tangible, crude, imperfect, alive. Momentum itself becomes a resource.

In those early days, conversation replaces documentation. Decisions are made standing up, not sitting in meetings. There is no "process," only purpose. The engineer who designs the circuit also tests it, markets it, and installs it. The same people who build the product also define the mission. Failure is frequent, but so is adaptation. These are the golden hours of creativity, the period when *doing feels easier than deciding*. Problems are puzzles, not liabilities; experiments are evidence, not risk. Every iteration carries the thrill of discovery and the freedom of speed. But success changes the physics of an organization. The first big order arrives, then the second, and with them come new expectations. Investors demand predictability. Customers demand reliability. Regulators demand documentation. Suddenly, the same speed that once built the company begins to look reckless. So, structures emerge, rational, necessary structures. A manager to coordinate projects, an accountant to track expenses, a legal advisor to manage contracts, or a compliance officer to "make sure we never get in trouble". Each addition seems sensible, even wise. But like sandbags piled against a flood, they accumulate until the current of creativity no longer moves.

The company grows in headcount, in systems, in meetings but something intangible begins to slow. Decisions that once took minutes now take weeks. Experiments need sign-offs. Conversations require calendar invites. The founder who once shouted across the room now needs a slide deck to make the same point. This transformation is almost invisible while it happens. It doesn't announce itself through failure or crisis; it settles quietly, like silt in a riverbed. The current remains, but it runs shallow. Layers of oversight, reporting, and approvals accumulate until movement itself feels heavy. What was once fluid becomes viscous. And so, the company that once thrived on improvisation now worships process. Where once engineers-built prototypes in a day, they now draft proposals that must clear three levels of management. Where once failure meant *learning*, it now means *liability*. Where once ideas competed in the open, they now wait in line for budget approval.

Eventually, the organization stops running on imagination and starts running on governance. The people are still smart, the goals are still ambitious, but the tempo is gone. The energy that once pulsed through late-night brainstorming sessions has been replaced by the hum of scheduled efficiency. Innovation is no longer a behavior, it's a department. And like all departments, it reports to someone, just another node in a network of approvals that ensures no one ever moves too fast again.

From Chaos to Control and Back Again

Every startup begins in chaos but it's a productive chaos, a kind that burns bright and fast. In those first years, structure feels like an obstacle. The team thrives on improvisation, intuition, and the kind of creative disorder that would terrify a corporate manager. Mistakes happen daily, but they are quickly corrected, and every setback adds to the collective intelligence of the group. There's a rhythm to it; messy, noisy, electric. Everyone wears five hats. Engineers debate strategy, marketers solder wires, and founders write code between investor calls. The lines between departments don't exist because there are no departments. It's an ecosystem of urgency, a living organism reacting and adapting in real time.

But success does something subtle, it introduces the illusion of permanence. Once the company finds a market, chaos becomes less romantic. Investors want forecasts, customers want guarantees, and leadership begins to crave predictability. The same spontaneity that once fueled growth now threatens stability. So begins the quiet revolution of control. A process is written to standardize what used to be improvised. A department is created to monitor what used to be trusted. A meeting is scheduled to discuss what used to be decided. The transition feels rational, even responsible. Every new rule, every approval step, is justified by some past mistake. Each new policy has a story behind it: a shipment delayed, a contract misfiled, a lawsuit narrowly avoided. Slowly, rules accumulate not to enable success, but to prevent blame.

In this new world, prevention becomes the measure of competence. Managers are rewarded for avoiding surprises, not for enabling breakthroughs. Teams that once asked, *"How do we make this work?"* now ask, *"Who needs to approve this?"* The organization shifts from seeking opportunity to managing risk.

And here lies the paradox: bureaucracy is not created by incompetence, but by intelligence misapplied. It is built by smart people solving yesterday's problems. Every safeguard, every form, every review was once a rational response to a real failure. But when multiplied, they form a labyrinth. No one meant to slow the company down, they simply wanted to protect it.

Soon, protection becomes identity. Aerospace firms that once chased the impossible landing on the moon, inventing stealth, now measure success in compliance scores. Medical-device companies once driven by human ingenuity now optimize for audit readiness. Tech firms that once boasted of "failing fast" now spend more time preparing documentation for meetings than writing code. Control becomes the new chaos, a self-perpetuating system that exists to justify itself. Meetings multiply because meetings already exist. Committees form to align committees. Every problem becomes a process, and every process is a policy.

When NASA launched the Apollo missions, it did so with slide rules, cigarettes, and a shared sense of purpose. Engineers made life-and-death decisions on the fly because they had to. Today, that same agency could take years to approve a new bolt design. The difference is not intelligence, it's inertia. Inside every mature organization, you can feel this weight. The spirit that once said, *"Let's try it,"* now says, *"Let's review it"*. The same courage that once embraced uncertainty is replaced by a culture that fears deviation. Every rule added to reduce risk quietly reduces speed.

And yet, even as companies drown in their own order, they rarely notice. They mistake motion for progress, the constant churn of meetings, memos, and metrics gives the illusion of productivity. But underneath, the current has slowed. It is in this moment when a company finally believes its processes are its product that the seeds of decline take root. From here, the bureaucracy will only grow heavier, denser, and harder to dismantle. The organization that once thrived on agility now survives on procedure, its success slowly strangled by the systems meant to preserve it.

The Tipping Point: When Order Becomes Obstacle

Every bureaucracy begins with reason. It doesn't appear as red tape, but as reassurance, a way to make success repeatable. After the chaos of early growth, structure feels like progress. Processes are written, responsibilities defined, approvals introduced. The goal is simple: to preserve what worked and prevent what failed. At first, it works beautifully. Documentation clarifies expectations. Reporting creates accountability. Procedures protect consistency. The company becomes reliable , not just fast, but *predictably* fast. Customers trust it. Investors praise it. Employees feel the comfort of rhythm. But somewhere along the way, that rhythm becomes rigidity. The very mechanisms designed to create order begin to demand it. Rules that once helped decisions move faster now make them heavier. Checks that once prevented chaos now prevent change.

It happens quietly, almost imperceptibly, the moment when structure stops serving people and people start serving structure. At first, bureaucracy is the scaffolding around growth. But like scaffolding left up too long, it starts to block the very building it was meant to support.

Each department, originally formed to solve a problem, becomes a gatekeeper for its own existence. Finance was meant to enable investment, now it restricts it. Legal was meant to protect the company, now it defines what's possible. Quality assurance was meant to guarantee excellence, now it demands evidence before imagination. Every process, every policy, every layer of review started as a fix for something that went wrong, a late delivery, a failed product, a lawsuit, a missed quarter. But rather than learning from these mistakes, organizations begin to *institutionalize* them. They treat every past failure as a prophecy, designing systems to make sure it never happens again and in doing so, they ensure that nothing surprising ever happens again either.

The tipping point is not a single moment; it's a gradual surrender. It's when a company's instinct to move turns into its instinct to monitor. When leadership stops asking, *"What should we build next?"* and starts asking, *"What went wrong last time?"* When meetings shift from creation to coordination, from "how do we do this?" to "who owns this?" This transition is often celebrated as "professionalization." The board calls it maturity. Consultants call it operational excellence. But to those who live inside it the engineers, the designers, the thinkers it feels like a tightening. Like oxygen slowly thinning in the air. The tipping point arrives when the organization begins optimizing for predictability instead of possibility. It's the moment when control, once the guardian of performance, becomes its jailer. The irony is that few notice it happening in real time. The metrics still look healthy. Revenue still grows. Products still ship. But the pulse has changed. Speed gives way to procedure. Urgency becomes protocol. And innovation, once the lifeblood of the company, becomes a managed event scheduled, reviewed, and approved like any other function. By the time anyone realizes what's been lost, bureaucracy has already woven itself into the DNA It's not a problem anymore, it's the culture. And culture, once ossified, resists every attempt to change it. This is how bureaucracy takes over: not through rebellion, but through repetition. Not by breaking the system, but by perfecting it.

The Creeping Layers of Management

Bureaucracy doesn't announce itself with fanfare; it arrives quietly, disguised as professionalism. At first, the layers of management feel like progress, a sign of maturity, of evolution. Titles multiply: project managers, division heads, senior directors, vice presidents of alignment. Each new layer is meant to coordinate, to clarify, to ensure that the right hand knows what the left hand is doing. But soon, everyone is watching everyone else, and no one is moving forward.

In the early days, decisions happen where the work happens. Engineers solve problems in real time. Designers test, iterate, and fix what's broken before anyone asks for a report. But as organizations grow, distance seeps in, not just physical distance, but cognitive and cultural. The people who make decisions no longer build things; the people who build things no longer make decisions.

At first, this separation feels harmless, even efficient. After all, executives can't be everywhere at once. But gradually, the distance becomes distortion. The message traveling up the hierarchy is polished, reframed, and sanitized at each level, until by the time it reaches the top, it bears little resemblance to reality. And when direction comes back down, it is diluted again, vague, risk-averse, and shaped more by optics than by understanding. The results are predictable: delay, confusion, and detachment. Meetings multiply not to solve problems, but to translate intent between layers. PowerPoint becomes the lingua franca of the disconnected. Everyone talks about alignment, but few notice how little actually moves.

Nowhere is this more visible or tragic than in the aerospace industry. Once, Boeing represented the purest expression of American engineering culture, bold, pragmatic, and deeply technical. Engineers sat a few doors away from factory floors. Decisions about safety, materials, and design were made by those who understood the physics, not just the profit margins. But by the late 1990s, after mergers and reorganizations, Boeing's DNA began to change. Finance started to outrank engineering. The company's headquarters moved a thousand miles away from its manufacturing base, a symbolic and literal separation between those who built and those who budgeted.

When the 737 MAX crisis unfolded, it wasn't just product deficiency, it was a management failure decades in the making. Engineers raised safety concerns about the aircraft's Maneuvering Characteristics Augmentation System (MCAS), but their warnings were either dismissed or buried under layers of management. As financial executives prioritized cost-cutting over engineering excellence, the company lost sight of its commitment to safety, leading to two fatal crashes and one of the biggest corporate scandals in aviation history.

This outcome stemmed from a series of internal decisions and cultural shifts that began over two decades earlier, eroding Boeing's once-renowned engineering ethos. The 1997 merger with McDonnell Douglas marked a pivotal turning point, introducing a cost-cutting mindset that clashed with Boeing's traditional focus on engineering excellence. Under CEO Philip Condit, who orchestrated the acquisition, the company began prioritizing short-term profits and shareholder value over long-term innovation and safety. This cultural drift intensified in 2001 when Condit relocated Boeing's headquarters from Seattle, its engineering heartland, to Chicago for tax incentives, physically and symbolically distancing executives from the engineers and production teams. As one analysis from Harvard Business School notes, this move alienated Seattle-based staff and shifted decision-making toward financial metrics rather than technical rigor.

Subsequent leadership changes further entrenched these priorities. Harry Stonecipher, a former McDonnell Douglas executive appointed CEO in 2003, explicitly aimed to transform Boeing, declaring, "When people say I changed the culture of Boeing, that was the intent, so that it's run like a business rather than a great engineering firm." His successor, Jim McNerney, a GE alumnus, opted in 2011 to upgrade the aging 737 model rather than design a new aircraft, responding to competitive pressure from Airbus's A320neo. This decision, driven by customer demands like Southwest Airlines' insistence on avoiding pilot retraining costs, led to rushed compromises: larger engines were mounted higher on the wings, creating aerodynamic instability that MCAS was meant to address. However, MCAS relied on a single angle-of-attack sensor without redundancy, a violation of standard aviation safety protocols, to cut costs and expedite certification.

Under CEO Dennis Muilenburg during the 2018 and 2019 crashes, safety oversights compounded. Engineers' concerns about MCAS were downplayed or siloed due to fragmented reporting structures, where project owners did not directly oversee technical teams. The Federal Aviation Administration (FAA) delegated much of the certification to Boeing under its Organization Designation Authorization program, creating conflicts of interest. As a congressional report later revealed, Boeing failed to fully disclose MCAS to pilots or regulators, treating it as a minor feature to avoid additional training expenses. Internal communications showed employees expressing alarm, with one engineer warning that the aggressive production schedule was "trying to do too much with too little," yet these voices were often ignored amid pressure to meet deadlines and boost stock performance.

Investigations, including a 2020 U.S. congressional report, attributed the tragedies, which claimed 346 lives, to a "slow but steady drift from a culture of engineering, safety, and value." The report highlighted how profit-driven incentives led to a "cozy" relationship with the FAA, eroded regulatory oversight, and fostered an environment where safety was subordinated to speed and cost savings. In response, Boeing admitted responsibility in legal settlements, but the crisis cost the company over $20 billion and damaged its reputation, underscoring the perils of a profit-over-people culture.

A similar trend is seen in defense contractors like Lockheed Martin and Raytheon, where risk-averse leadership often delays promising defense technologies due to lengthy approval processes and strict compliance frameworks. Each layer did its job, approving, reviewing, documenting and in doing so, ensured that no one was accountable. The distance between those who knew the danger and those who could act on it proved fatal.

This is how bureaucratic layering works: it spreads responsibility so thin that it disappears. No single decision is ever entirely wrong, but the sum of them is disastrous. And the pattern repeats across industries. At Google, world-class researchers in artificial intelligence produce breakthroughs that rarely see daylight because product approvals must pass through multiple committees balancing brand risk, legal exposure, and internal politics. At NASA, engineers lament that it takes years to approve a hardware change that used to take weeks during Apollo. At Lockheed Martin, talented young designers leave for startups like Relativity Space or Rocket Lab, tired of waiting for "review cycles" that outlast their patience.

Layering also alters incentives. In a flat, fast-moving company, success is measured by output by what you build, ship, or learn. In a layered one, success is measured by perception, how smoothly your projects appear to run, how well your reports align with the strategy, how convincingly you justify your budget. Appearance replaces achievement. The best presenters rise faster than the best performers.

Middle management, once a bridge between leadership and execution, becomes a buffer. Its purpose shifts from enabling teams to protecting them or protecting leadership from bad news. Over time, this protective reflex calcifies into resistance. Instead of asking "How do we move faster?" middle managers ask, "What will this mean for my department?" Instead of collaborating to solve a problem, they negotiate ownership of it.

This structural drag produces a cultural effect that is even more dangerous: detachment. When senior leaders see their organization only through dashboards, metrics, and slide decks, they begin managing abstractions instead of people. They lose touch with the texture of the work, the hum of the lab, the pulse of the factory, the excitement of engineers solving real problems. They manage performance indicators, not performance. Over time, this detachment breeds cynicism below and complacency above. Front-line innovators learn that enthusiasm is naïve, that bold ideas die in layers. Executives, insulated by numbers, believe the system is stable, until it suddenly isn't.

The tragedy is that everyone inside knows what's happening, but no one feels authorized to change it. Each layer depends on the one above it, and the one above depends on the system itself. It's a perfectly self-reinforcing machine one that produces predictability at the cost of progress. By the time a company realizes it has too many layers, those layers have become its identity. Removing them feels dangerous, like performing surgery on oneself. So they remain outlasting CEOs, strategies, and crises until innovation has nowhere left to go but out the door. And that's exactly what happens. The most ambitious people leave. They go where ideas can still breathe to smaller firms, to startups, or sometimes to competitors unburdened by heritage. They take with them not just their talent, but their urgency.

What's left behind is the most stable version of decline: a company that runs perfectly, predictably, and painfully slowly.

Process as a Religion

Every bureaucracy begins with a noble intention: to prevent chaos. But somewhere along the way, the tools designed to guide progress become objects of worship. Rules, procedures, and protocols, once instruments of efficiency, are elevated into unquestionable truths.

Inside mature corporations, process stops serving innovation and starts defining it. The question shifts subtly but decisively from *"Does this work?"* to *"Did we follow the process?"* It's not about whether the solution is good, but whether the steps taken were correct. The path becomes more important than the destination. You can see this mindset everywhere, in meetings that exist to prepare for other meetings, in approval workflows that require half a dozen signatures for decisions no one will ever challenge, in project updates that measure adherence rather than advancement. There's a quiet comfort in it. Processes promise fairness, predictability, safety, and all the things that chaos once threatened. But they also erase spontaneity, flatten curiosity, and punish urgency. ·

In the early days of a company, a process is a shared memory. It's something the team invents together after learning from a mistake: *"Next time, let's do it this way."* But as the organization scales, process becomes law, something inherited, not created. No one remembers *why* it exists; only that it must. An engineer might ask, "Why do we need three signatures to run a test?" and the answer, inevitably, is, "That's how it's always been done." A marketing lead might wonder, "Why do we wait for quarterly reviews to approve new campaigns?" and the answer is, "That's our process." Process becomes its own justification, self-sustaining belief system that exists to sustain itself. The irony is that in trying to remove human error, companies remove human judgment. The more automated and codified a decision becomes, the less space there is for intuition, creativity, or courage. People stop thinking and start complying. They do things not because they make sense, but because not doing them feels dangerous.

In one large aerospace company, a team of engineers waited six months to test a new material for a critical component, not because the science was uncertain, but because the vendor wasn't on the "approved supplier list." The engineers petitioned for an exception.

The request bounced between departments, accumulating signatures and revisions until the opportunity passed. By the time approval arrived, a competitor had already filed a patent on the same concept.

In the medical-device industry, similar stories unfold daily. A brilliant new diagnostic technology can languish for years, entangled in overlapping reviews from engineering, legal, and regulatory teams, each performing its role perfectly, each ensuring that no one is to blame. When the project is finally released, the market has moved on. The product arrives on time, by the company's internal calendar, but years too late for the world outside.

This is how process becomes religion, not because anyone decrees it, but because everyone quietly agrees to it. In the absence of speed, the illusion of order becomes sacred. Following procedure becomes the moral high ground. Breaking it, even for the sake of progress, becomes heresy. You can feel it in the language: People start saying "compliance" more than "creativity." They measure "throughput" instead of impact. They celebrate "alignment" rather than originality. The organization develops a liturgy, acronyms, templates, and dashboards that give form to its rituals.

Within this system, the innovators are not heroes; they are heretics. The ones who ask uncomfortable questions are labeled "unstructured." The ones who move fast are told to slow down "for everyone's safety." And so, slowly but surely, the company begins to select against its own innovators.

At IBM in the late 1980s, engineers who once built the personal computer revolution found themselves trapped in an increasingly process-driven machine. Internal committees reviewed everything, from component choices to language in user manuals. A simple decision could require approval from multiple vice presidents, each guarding their jurisdiction. As bureaucracy tightened its grip, creative engineers left to join smaller, faster firms, Apple, Sun Microsystems, and a thousand startups that would shape the digital era. IBM had the talent, the capital, and the technology. What it lacked was permission to move. The same story echoes today in companies across industries. A medical conglomerate measures the success of its R&D team not by patents or breakthroughs but by audit-readiness. A defense contractor congratulates itself for "zero non-compliances" in a project that has missed its delivery date by two years. A tech giant celebrates an "alignment milestone" while startups release products that make the milestone irrelevant.

The tragedy of process is that it feels virtuous. Everyone inside the system believes they are doing the right thing, protecting quality, ensuring fairness, reducing risk. But beneath that virtue lies stagnation. When process becomes religion, innovation becomes ritual, predictable, ceremonial, and hollow. The organization still holds meetings about creativity, still funds "innovation initiatives," still hires consultants to teach design thinking. But the energy that once came from discovery has been replaced by the comfort of procedure.

And like all religions, bureaucracy demands devotion, not to results, but to faith in the system itself. It rewards the obedient, elevates the cautious, and exiles the impatient. It converts progress into paperwork and boldness into policy. Somewhere along the line, the question changes. It's no longer *"What can we build next?"* It's *"Who signed off on this?"* That's when a company knows it has crossed the invisible line, when process no longer protects innovation but imprisons it. And yet, inside the walls, few notice. The rituals continue, the metrics are met, and the reports glow with green indicators. On paper, the company looks perfectly healthy. But in spirit, it has already begun to die.

The Fear Economy Inside the Enterprise

Fear is bureaucracy's invisible currency. It doesn't appear in budgets or reports, but it shapes everything. Fear of failure. Fear of blame. Fear of standing out. These fears are what keep the machinery running, polished, compliant, and utterly predictable.

When a company grows large enough, its employees stop working *for* success and start working *against* failure. The difference is subtle but transformative. In a creative culture, people chase opportunity; in a bureaucratic one, they chase safety. Every idea is filtered through a quiet mental equation: *What happens to me if this goes wrong?* At first, this fear manifests as caution, a delay here, an extra review there. But soon, it becomes the operating system of the organization. Meetings fill with hedging language: "Let's revisit this," "We need alignment," "Legal should look at it first." Each phrase feels harmless, but collectively they translate to one thing: *not yet*. And "not yet" becomes the company's unofficial motto.

Inside the fear economy, people learn new forms of survival. They don't stop innovating entirely, they just innovate invisibly. Ideas are kept small, safe, and familiar enough to avoid scrutiny. Managers, trained by years of organizational politics, learn to disguise ambition as pragmatism. Teams pursue projects that can't fail rather than projects that might succeed spectacularly.

At GE Healthcare, for example, engineers once at the forefront of medical imaging began to hesitate when AI entered the field. They had the expertise, the data, and the brand to lead. But AI was untested territory, full of regulatory uncertainty. A failed pilot could mean public embarrassment, investor skepticism, or worse, job loss. So the company waited. Meanwhile, Siemens and Philips moved forward, releasing AI-driven systems that redefined diagnostics. GE didn't fall because it lacked innovation; it fell because it was afraid to use it. Fear changes incentives in subtle, corrosive ways. In fast-moving organizations, people are rewarded for what they create. In bureaucracies, they're rewarded for what they prevent. The hero is no longer the one who takes the bold step, but the one who avoids the mistake. Risk-takers become liabilities. Gatekeepers become leaders. Promotion pathways reflect this inversion. Those who never cause trouble rise quickly. The quiet, compliant, and careful are trusted with authority. Over time, this produces a culture of managers who don't lead, they supervise. Their job is to make sure nothing unexpected happens. And so, nothing does.

When fear takes root, the organization's collective IQ begins to fall, not because its people are less capable, but because they stop thinking boldly. Engineers start designing for compliance instead of performance. Marketers design campaigns that won't offend. Executives speak in abstractions that can't be proven wrong. The company's energy shifts from *creating* value to *protecting* it, from expansion to preservation. Even success becomes something to fear, because success raises expectations, and expectations increase risk. People learn to aim just low enough to guarantee survival.

This fear-driven inertia is most visible in how companies talk about mistakes. In small startups, a failed prototype is dissected, laughed about, and replaced by a better one the next morning. In large corporations, failure requires a postmortem, a root-cause analysis, and sometimes, a reorganization. It isn't just a learning moment, it's an event. And the lesson everyone absorbs isn't how to improve, but how to avoid being in that report next time.

Over years, this mindset creates a paradoxical environment, one of hyper-accountability without real accountability. Every error is documented, but no one is responsible. Every risk is managed, but nothing is ventured. It's a perfect equilibrium of self-preservation and stagnation. Nowhere is this dynamic more visible than in the aerospace and defense sectors, where the stakes are highest and the fear most institutionalized. An engineer proposing a design improvement must navigate countless "what ifs", not just technical ones, but political, contractual, and bureaucratic. A single misstep could delay a program, trigger audits, or invite congressional scrutiny. So, engineers stop proposing.

In one major defense firm, a project manager once joked that "the fastest way to get fired is to do something new." Everyone laughed, but no one disagreed. The result is a kind of slow-motion paralysis: projects advance, but only within the safest boundaries. Everyone follows the rules, everyone covers their tracks, and nothing truly innovative gets built.

Fear doesn't just control decisions, it rewires identity. It teaches people to value perception over performance. To keep their heads down, stay in the middle, and never volunteer for uncertainty. Over time, this conformity becomes self-sustaining. Employees don't need to be told to play it safe; they've internalized the algorithm.

Walk through the halls of any large corporation, and you can feel it, a quiet, professional anxiety disguised as calm. Everyone is busy, but no one is daring. The walls are covered with motivational posters about innovation, but the only thing that moves fast is email. It's a culture where people smile in meetings but exhale in private. Where ambition feels like risk, and silence feels like wisdom.

The cruel irony is that fear looks like order from the outside. To investors, regulators, and even the board, the company appears healthy, predictable margins, consistent deliverables, no surprises. But beneath that glossy stability lies decay. No one takes risks, no one learns, and no one leads. A company that once pulsed with creative tension now hums with quiet compliance. It's efficient, but lifeless, perfectly structured to avoid disaster and therefore incapable of achieving greatness.

This is the final evolution of bureaucracy: when the desire for safety becomes indistinguishable from the fear of movement. A culture so preoccupied with avoiding mistakes that it forgets how to make progress. And yet, this isn't the end of the story, not yet. Because beneath that stillness, something else begins to stir: the cost of fear. The engineers who still dream of speed. The managers who remember what agility once felt like. The innovators who realize that *not failing* has quietly become the same as *not trying*. They are the ones who will either leave, or, if the company is lucky, fight to reclaim what it lost. But before they can, they must confront the final and most visible manifestation of bureaucracy, not in rules or structures, but in regulation itself. That's where the next phase of stagnation begins: when caution becomes strategy, and compliance becomes the ultimate product.

Regulatory Paralysis: When Caution Becomes the Strategy

If fear is bureaucracy's heartbeat, regulation is its armor, the layer that hardens around it and makes change almost impossible. What begins as an internal preference for safety becomes an external justification for stagnation. Regulation provides the perfect defense: *We're not slow; we're compliant.* And in industries where lives, safety, or public trust are at stake, that defense is unassailable.

But over time, something subtle happens. Regulation, designed to protect the public, becomes a convenient excuse to protect the organization. Caution stops being a temporary posture and becomes the strategy itself. In theory, regulation exists to ensure fairness and safety. In practice, it often enshrines bureaucracy. Every rule spawns a department to interpret it, a committee to enforce it, and a culture to fear it. What starts as accountability becomes ritualized caution, a belief that speed is synonymous with recklessness and that innovation without a checklist is heresy.

Inside large corporations, entire teams exist not to create, but to anticipate regulators. They write policies no one reads, maintain documentation no one questions, and design processes to prove that every decision, even the smallest one, left a trail of signatures. The company becomes less concerned with what it builds and more obsessed with how it would look in an audit. Executives reassure themselves that this is discipline. But discipline without direction is paralysis.

Nowhere is this paralysis more visible than in the medical-device industry. Here, the fear of noncompliance has all but replaced the drive for discovery. A new diagnostic technology, capable of saving lives, can spend five to seven years in bureaucratic limbo before reaching a patient. By the time it does, the science has evolved, the competitors have moved on, and the innovators who conceived it have long since left the company.

At one major manufacturer, engineers described the approval process for a single product change as "a project in itself." A new feature needed validation through engineering, regulatory, legal, and clinical teams, each working in sequence rather than collaboration. Months turned into years, not because the technology failed, but because the paperwork never stopped moving. The engineers joked darkly: "We move at the speed of signatures." Meanwhile, startups outside the system iterate freely. They test, fail, learn, and improve faster than the large firms can schedule a meeting. By the time the corporate giant is ready to launch, the startup has already launched five times and been acquired by someone else.

The aerospace industry tells the same story, only with higher altitudes and higher stakes. Safety regulations are essential, no one questions that. But when safety becomes synonymous with stagnation, the mission itself begins to suffer. In the 1960s, NASA sent men to the moon using analog computers, slide rules, and courage. Today, a single redesign of a bolt or a panel can take years to approve, not because engineers are less capable, but because the approval ecosystem is infinitely heavier. For every hour of design, there are days of documentation; for every test, weeks of review. Boeing's Starliner capsule, conceived to restore America's human spaceflight capability, has endured year after year of delay, a victim of overlapping oversight, redundant checks, and constant re-certification cycles. Meanwhile, SpaceX, operating with a fraction of the bureaucracy, launched, landed, and reused rockets in the same timeframe. Both companies are bound by the same laws of physics, but only one is bound by the laws of its own caution.

The pharmaceutical industry suffers from an even deeper form of paralysis, one written into its DNA. Developing a new drug now takes an average of 10 to 15 years and costs upward of $2.5 billion. Only about one in ten candidates that enter human trials ever reach the market. The rest die in paperwork, not because they're unsafe, but because they can't survive the financial and regulatory gauntlet that modern pharma has built around itself. For decades, researchers pursued mRNA vaccine technology with promising results, yet no one dared push it forward. The risk of failure, regulatory, financial, reputational, was simply too high. It took a global emergency to break the stalemate. Once the world was desperate, regulators moved faster than ever before. Clinical trials overlapped instead of proceeding sequentially. Approvals that once took years were granted in months. And what was revealed was shocking, the obstacle had never been the science; it had been the system. The same technology that "wasn't ready" for thirty years suddenly saved millions of lives when bureaucracy was forced to step aside. If that's not proof of regulatory inertia, what is?

Even finance, the supposed engine of innovation in the global economy, is captive to its own compliance culture. Large banks and insurers, armed with thousands of lawyers and risk officers, have built fortresses of procedure so high that innovation can't climb over them. Every new idea, from blockchain to AI-driven credit scoring, must pass through an endless circuit of committees asking the same question: *What could go wrong?* By the time the answer is satisfactory, the question is obsolete. In contrast, FinTech startups like Stripe, Square, and Revolut emerged precisely because they were born outside that fortress. They embraced managed risk, navigated evolving regulation creatively, and moved at the speed of user need. Traditional institutions watched from behind their compliance walls, comforted by their prudence, until they realized prudence had cost them relevance.

Across all these industries, a grim pattern emerges: Regulation, once a safeguard, becomes a shield behind which bureaucracy hides. Every delay, every inefficiency, every missed opportunity can be explained away with one sentence: *We're following the rules.* But when rules multiply endlessly, they stop protecting the public and start protecting mediocrity. The system teaches organizations that the safest decision is no decision at all. And so, leaders delay, teams over-document, and employees lose the ability to distinguish between real risk and bureaucratic risk. Innovation doesn't die in confrontation, it dies in compliance. The irony is that many of these companies know they are stuck. Their executives deliver conference speeches about agility and digital transformation. They form "innovation councils," launch "accelerators," and hire "chief transformation officers." But even these attempts are swallowed by the same system they seek to change. The accelerator needs legal approval. The council needs governance. The chief transformation officer needs a steering committee.

And so, the bureaucracy learns to reinvent itself in the language of reform. It adapts, absorbs, and survives, like a living organism protecting its host. By this stage, caution has fully evolved into strategy. Speed is treated as recklessness; experimentation as irresponsibility. The organization convinces itself that it's protecting value, when in truth it's protecting its own structure. This is regulatory paralysis: the point at which companies no longer need external constraints, they have internalized them. They think like regulators even when no one is watching.

The tragedy is not that regulation exists, but that innovation has learned to fear it. And the greatest danger isn't the rules we're forced to follow, it's the ones we impose on ourselves.

The Decision-Making Gridlock

Inside every large organization lies a paradox: the bigger it grows, the more talent it hires, yet the less capable it becomes of making a decision. Every department is full of expertise, every meeting full of intelligence, every report full of data, and yet, momentum disappears. The gears of the company still turn, but they turn without traction. The problem isn't ignorance; it's diffusion. Responsibility, once clear, becomes a cloud. Every choice is everyone's job, and therefore no one's.

In a small company, decision-making is visceral. You can feel the pulse of the business through the people in the room. If something breaks, you fix it. If a customer complains, you change the design. The line between awareness and action is almost nonexistent. But in a large corporation, awareness and action exist on different planets. An engineer discovers a flaw but must report it through a chain. A manager recognizes an opportunity but needs cross-functional alignment. An executive sees a market shift but waits for quarterly strategy reviews. By the time the company decides, the world has already moved on.

This is not indecision, it's decision gridlock, a paralysis created by abundance: too many opinions, too many approvals, too many stakeholders who must sign off before anything can happen. Meetings multiply to coordinate other meetings. Subcommittees form to clarify what the main committee meant. Email threads stretch into novels. And somewhere in that bureaucratic sprawl, the urgency that once defined the company quietly dissolves. The organization becomes like an orchestra where every musician waits for permission to play. You can see this dynamic most clearly in industries once defined by decisive leadership, technology, aerospace, and defense.

At Intel, once the undisputed king of microprocessors, engineers spent years warning leadership about the architectural limits of their chips. They proposed bold redesigns to catch up to rivals like AMD and Apple. But rather than choose a direction, Intel's committees debated endlessly, balancing risk models, budget scenarios, and political considerations between business units. Each meeting ended with the same phrase: *"We need more data."* By the time the data arrived, it was irrelevant. Competitors had already made the leap. Intel didn't lose because it lacked genius, it lost because it no longer knew how to decide.

The same pattern haunts legacy giants like Microsoft, IBM, and HP, all of which once set the pace of global innovation but eventually fell victim to their own deliberative gravity. In the mid-2000s, Microsoft engineers knew mobile computing would define the future. They built prototypes, presented roadmaps, even ran pilot programs. But each new direction had to pass through product committees, legal reviews, and marketing councils. The organization debated endlessly about how to avoid cannibalizing its existing Windows franchise. When it finally acted, Apple and Google had already taken the field. Inside Microsoft, the joke became grimly prophetic: *"We never miss a meeting."*

Decision gridlock is more than procedural; it's cultural. When employees see that bold decisions are punished while cautious ones are rewarded, they learn to wait. When they notice that bad outcomes result in reorganizations while delayed outcomes result in nothing, they choose delay. The company gradually becomes a maze of polite avoidance, a place where meetings end with conclusions like, *"Let's align next week,"* or *"We'll revisit this after leadership weighs in."*

No one means to slow things down. Everyone believes they're being responsible. But responsibility without courage produces inertia, and inertia, in the world of innovation, is death by professionalism. The decision-making process itself becomes performative. Executives expect data-driven rigor, so teams bury them in data. Boards demand governance, so management builds layers of review. Analysts request clarity, so leaders produce frameworks, models, and color-coded matrices. The output looks impressive: long reports, detailed presentations, complex charts. But none of it makes the company faster. It makes it *feel* safe while ensuring it never moves. This illusion of progress, motion without momentum, is one of bureaucracy's cruelest tricks. It convinces smart people that they're being thorough when, in reality, they're just being slow.

In the aerospace sector, this paralysis is legendary. At NASA, engineers joke that it now takes longer to approve a test than it once did to build a rocket. A single change to a design may require approval from multiple risk boards, quality review panels, and compliance officers, all of whom must agree, yet none of whom have the authority to decide. It's not that the system is broken, it's that it works exactly as designed: no single person can make a mistake, and therefore no one can make a move.

That's how decision gridlock works: it replaces accountability with documentation. The gridlock extends beyond engineering into leadership itself. When a CEO can't make a decision without aligning a dozen senior vice presidents, and those vice presidents can't act without aligning their divisions, the entire organization begins to orbit itself, spinning endlessly around questions of process, territory, and consensus.

At this point, time ceases to be an asset. It becomes a tax. Every day spent deciding is a day competitors spend advancing. And yet, to the bureaucratic mind, delay feels safer than decision.

You can almost chart the progression of decay:

- **The company stops deciding in the room.** Decisions are deferred for "review."
- **Accountability becomes collective.** Everyone owns the outcome, so no one owns it.
- **Speed is redefined as recklessness.** Those who push for urgency are labeled impatient or "not strategic."
- **Consensus becomes currency.** Getting everyone to agree becomes the goal, even if that agreement produces mediocrity.

By the time the organization realizes it's trapped, the gridlock has become culture. People confuse deliberation with diligence. Leaders conflate avoiding mistakes with creating value.

The company has achieved perfect equilibrium, steady, quiet, and directionless. The cost of this paralysis is often invisible until it's irreversible. Market share erodes quietly. Talent leaves gradually. Competitors rise suddenly. And by the time the board demands answers, the organization has lost something that no process can restore, *its instinct for movement.*

The most dangerous part of decision gridlock is that it feels responsible. Every delay is justified by good reasons, risk management, alignment, compliance, stakeholder input. But history rarely remembers the reasons we hesitated. It remembers the opportunities we missed.

In the end, no company is destroyed by indecision in a single moment. It's destroyed by a thousand postponed decisions, each small enough to seem reasonable at the time. And so, the enterprise that once prided itself on precision and discipline ends up paralyzed by them, a monument to its own caution. It doesn't collapse; it calcifies.

That's the quiet tragedy of bureaucracy: it doesn't die dramatically. It just stops moving.

The Consensus Mirage

When decision-making slows to a crawl, the next natural instinct is to seek comfort in consensus. If no one wants to be wrong, then everyone must agree, and if everyone agrees, no one can be blamed. It sounds reasonable, even noble. Collaboration, inclusivity, alignment, these are words that adorn mission statements and corporate retreats. But beneath their warmth lies a quiet pathology: the belief that innovation must be unanimous.

Consensus feels democratic, but it functions as a veto system. It doesn't elevate the best ideas, it dilutes them. Every sharp edge is rounded off, every bold claim softened, every unconventional thought reformatted into a language everyone can live with. The result is a culture of careful compromise, ideas engineered to offend no one and inspire no one.

In small, hungry teams, disagreement is oxygen. People argue, challenge, and test each other's ideas because the mission matters more than anyone's ego. But in large corporations, disagreement is political. It's seen not as creative friction but as a threat to harmony. Managers learn to nod publicly and disagree privately. Committees avoid tension because tension slows approval. And so, rather than confront hard truths, organizations learn to smooth them over. The meeting ends not with a decision, but with a statement: *"We're all on the same page."* It sounds productive, but sameness is not alignment, and silence is not consensus. Inside this environment, risk is social, not technical. It's safer to agree with a mediocre plan than to defend a better one that might fail. People start using consensus as armor: *If we all decided together, no one can be blamed.* Soon, every decision requires universal comfort, and every proposal is pre-filtered to ensure it won't disrupt that comfort.

When Nokia's engineers proposed early touchscreen smartphones in the early 2000s, they met this wall of consensus. Yes, the prototype worked. Yes, the user experience was revolutionary. But the leadership team, representing marketing, supply chain, finance, and software, wanted "alignment." Each department saw risk: production complexity, higher costs, uncertain market adoption. Rather than pick a direction, the company picked safety. They agreed, unanimously, to wait. Apple and Google didn't. Consensus killed Nokia not through conflict, but through agreement.

Consensus culture also reshapes how companies talk. You can hear it in the vocabulary of large organizations, the soft, careful language designed to avoid commitment:

- "Let's explore this further."
- "We need to ensure cross-functional buy-in."
- "Let's table this until we have more input."

These phrases are the corporate equivalent of tranquilizers. They make meetings feel calm and constructive while draining them of urgency.

The illusion of teamwork replaces the discomfort of truth. And over time, this illusion becomes addictive, because it feels good. Everyone leaves the room feeling validated, respected, and aligned. The fact that nothing actually moved forward is beside the point.

At Google, some teams quietly refer to this phenomenon as "alignment theater." A product idea might require sign-offs from design, engineering, marketing, privacy, ethics, and legal, all of which must "feel comfortable" before launch. The goal isn't to make something great; it's to make something that no one inside the company dislikes. And because no one dislikes it, no one outside the company loves it.

Even brilliant technologies, like advanced language models, AR systems, or health-tracking features, can spend years trapped in this alignment loop. The company's greatest threat isn't competition; it's agreement.

Consensus also breeds another subtle killer of innovation: false harmony. Teams begin to self-censor before they even speak. Junior employees learn to read the emotional temperature of a room before voicing an idea. Middle managers preemptively edit their proposals to match what they believe leadership wants to hear. Even senior executives stop challenging one another, afraid that visible conflict might signal weakness.

Soon, the company's collective intelligence begins to flatten. It stops thinking dynamically and starts thinking diplomatically. Its conversations sound polished but sterile, like meetings between people who've already decided not to disagree.

The tragedy of the consensus mirage is that it doesn't feel like failure. From the outside, everything looks perfect: Meetings are polite. Emails are professional. Slides are color-coded. Everyone agrees on the mission. Everyone supports the strategy. But that harmony is hollow, a stillness mistaken for strength.

History is merciless toward this kind of comfort. When a company stops arguing, it stops evolving. The absence of conflict is not the presence of health; it's the symptom of decay. Look at Kodak, where internal teams all agreed that digital photography was "the future," but also agreed that it "wasn't the right time." Or BlackBerry, where executives unanimously decided that physical keyboards were a non-negotiable customer expectation. They reached perfect alignment, right up until the market proved them perfectly wrong.

Consensus kills innovation not by force, but by kindness. It replaces confrontation with accommodation, clarity with compromise. It rewards diplomacy over dissent, presentation over progress. And perhaps most insidious of all, it leaves no fingerprints. No one gets blamed for the idea that never launched, the market that was never entered, the opportunity that quietly slipped away. After all, *everyone agreed.*

The pursuit of consensus becomes the organization's final stage of self-restraint. By now, fear, process, and caution have converged into a single behavior: stillness. The company no longer resists change, it simply never notices it arriving.

This is the ultimate illusion of bureaucracy: a structure that feels stable right up until it breaks. And when it finally does, the leaders look back in disbelief, at the endless meetings, the perfect reports, the calm assurances, and realize that the danger was never conflict. The danger was peace.

The Tyranny of the Short Term

If bureaucracy is the disease within, Wall Street is the environment that lets it spread. Even the most inwardly bloated organizations might still fight for renewal, if they weren't being constantly rewarded for standing still.

Modern corporations don't live on curiosity or courage; they live on quarterly earnings. Every 90 days, they face judgment, not from customers or engineers, but from investors, analysts, and algorithms. The question isn't, *"Are we building something great?"* It's, *"Did we hit the number?"* And so, the cadence of innovation, long, uncertain, experimental, collides with the cadence of finance, short, measurable, immediate. The long view shrinks to a fiscal quarter. Vision becomes a slide deck. Leadership becomes performance management for shareholders.

It wasn't always this way. In the mid-20th century, companies like IBM, AT&T Bell Labs, and GE invested in research that might not pay off for decades. They built laboratories, funded scientists, and chased impossible problems because they believed in technological destiny, that progress itself was the business model.

Bell Labs invented the transistor, the laser, and information theory, the bedrock of the modern world, without ever knowing which division would profit from it. IBM developed the first hard drives and programming languages before anyone could predict a commercial return. These companies made decisions measured in years, not quarters. They built the future because they could afford to wait for it.

But over time, that patience disappeared. The financialization of corporate culture, the rise of stock options, activist investors, and short-term performance bonuses, rewired the incentives. Innovation became a cost center. R&D was no longer an investment; it was an expense.

This shift created a profound inversion: The internal bureaucracy that once stifled creativity found reinforcement from the outside. Wall Street's quarterly hunger validated the very behaviors that made corporations slow. Caution became not only safe, it became profitable.

An executive who cancels an experimental project can point to higher margins. A CEO who cuts long-term R&D spending can boast about "discipline." Boards cheer efficiency metrics and cash reserves while competitors quietly build the next generation of technology.

In this system, even success becomes suspect. A visionary idea that doesn't yield revenue within a few quarters is labeled "unfocused." A bold acquisition that requires time to mature is called "dilutive." Every decision must fit neatly inside a reporting cycle that punishes the long view. This short-term obsession explains why so many corporations die not from failure, but from starvation, from a deliberate refusal to feed their future.

General Electric once symbolized innovation itself. Under Jack Welch, it became the archetype of financial engineering, spinning off R&D-heavy divisions, optimizing for earnings per share, and promoting leaders who mastered spreadsheets, not breakthroughs. The company's market value soared, until, inevitably, it collapsed under the weight of its own efficiency. GE didn't run out of ideas; it ran out of patience.

The same pattern played out at IBM, which spent billions on stock buybacks while competitors, Amazon, Google, Microsoft, poured those billions into cloud computing and AI. Wall Street rewarded IBM's restraint until it became irreversible decline. It was a perfect loop: bureaucracy created slowness, markets rewarded slowness, and innovation suffocated quietly between them.

The tyranny of the short term isn't limited to industrial giants; it's everywhere. Pharmaceutical companies abandon promising research because the trials might take too long to yield results. Automotive companies delay electric innovation until regulations force them. Tech giants hoard cash rather than risk volatile new markets. Even when they claim to innovate, their announcements are timed for investor calls, not for customers.

The real innovation happens elsewhere, in startups, universities, and skunkworks teams, where there's no investor call to prepare for, no quarterly review to survive. Short-termism seeps into the culture like moisture into wood. Managers start thinking in quarters. Teams plan in fiscal years. Nobody dreams in decades anymore. And when a leader dares to think long-term, they are quietly reminded that "the market won't understand."

The result is an economy of brilliant corporations that can't remember how to build things that last. They talk about vision but operate like day traders. They measure success not by what they've created, but by how predictably they can report it. Innovation, once the art of imagining what doesn't yet exist, becomes the science of forecasting what already does.

And yet, this cycle persists because it feels rational. Shareholders want returns. Executives want bonuses. Everyone is rewarded for short-term performance and insulated from long-term consequence. But history is cruel to rationality. Rational decisions, multiplied by millions of cautious managers, create irrational outcomes, stagnant industries, hollow giants, and lost decades of progress.

Look at Kodak, Nokia, BlackBerry, GE, Boeing, all of them victims not of bad ideas, but of good numbers. Their quarterly reports were immaculate, right up until the moment they weren't.

The tyranny of the short term completes bureaucracy's transformation. Fear, process, and consensus find their final justification in profit. The organization no longer needs to explain why it's slow, the stock price explains it for them.

Every system that could once challenge the culture of caution, engineering, design, research, imagination, is now subordinate to finance. Innovation doesn't die because it's wrong. It dies because it's late. And lateness, in a quarterly world, is failure.

This is the quiet pact between bureaucracy and the market: You protect me from risk; I protect you from volatility. You deliver predictability, I deliver reward. Together, we will keep the numbers smooth, the graphs upward, and the future postponed indefinitely.

It's an agreement that works, until it doesn't. Because while bureaucracies debate and markets applaud, someone else is always building. And by the time the giants realize it, the world has already moved on.

The Human Cost of Bureaucracy

For all its forms, charts, and balance sheets, bureaucracy's greatest casualty is not speed or profit, it's people. It doesn't destroy them dramatically. It erodes them quietly. Inside every large organization are brilliant minds who once joined with the promise of purpose. Engineers who wanted to build something that mattered. Scientists who wanted to push the boundaries of knowledge. Designers who believed they could change how people live, work, and connect. They arrive full of ambition, curiosity, and defiance, and for a while, those qualities serve them well. Then, slowly, imperceptibly, the system begins to teach them how to survive. At first, it's subtle. An idea gets delayed "until next quarter." A meeting runs out of time before decisions are made. A proposal gets revised, re-scoped, and reconsidered until it no longer resembles the original vision.

The message is never stated outright, but it's clear: move carefully, stay aligned, don't stand out. The young engineer learns to soften bold ideas before presenting them. The scientist learns to hide controversial findings until the political climate improves. The manager learns to spend more time reporting progress than making it.

Over time, imagination is replaced by caution. Passion turns into patience. People stop asking, *"What if?"* and start asking, *"Is this approved?"* The organization, once alive with restless curiosity, becomes a place where everyone is busy but few are fulfilled.

Walk through the halls of any major corporation and you can see it in the faces, the quiet professionalism, the polite detachment. People are careful with their words, deferential in meetings, fluent in the language of safety. They know which projects will be rewarded and which will be "too risky." They can sense which ideas will sail through approval and which will die without explanation.

The tragedy is that most of them are still capable of greatness. They still carry the same instincts that once made the company vibrant, creativity, impatience, urgency. But those instincts now exist in a culture that treats them as liabilities. Every act of boldness must first survive a ritual of justification: *What's the ROI? What's the precedent? Who's responsible if it fails?* Eventually, most people stop volunteering their courage. The system wins, not through coercion, but through exhaustion.

It's not just ambition that fades; it's craftsmanship. When decisions are made by committees, individuals stop owning outcomes. When success depends on approval, integrity gives way to compliance. When process replaces judgment, people forget how to trust their instincts.

The best engineers stop arguing for better solutions and settle for approved ones. The best designers stop fighting for elegance and start optimizing for policy. The best scientists stop challenging assumptions and start documenting them.

They don't leave immediately; they adapt. They learn to navigate politics, to deliver what's asked, to "manage upward." And in doing so, they slowly become what the system rewards: reliable, agreeable, replaceable.

For those who can't adapt, there's only one option, escape. That's why startups are filled not with inexperience, but with exiles. They're populated by people who could no longer breathe inside the slow, polished corridors of corporate life. They leave not just to chase opportunity, but to recover their agency, to feel again what it's like to decide, to build, to move.

Every wave of innovation begins with these refugees of bureaucracy: engineers from Boeing joining SpaceX, developers from IBM joining Google, executives from conglomerates launching small, focused ventures of their own. They leave behind stability for uncertainty, because in uncertainty, there's life.

But not everyone escapes. Most stay, quietly. They have mortgages, families, reputations. They're good at what they do, and the system still needs them. So they learn to make peace with the inertia. They convince themselves that their contribution is to keep things running, that stewardship is enough.

And perhaps it is. Not every company can be a startup. Not every person wants to live in chaos. But when enough people surrender to stability, the organization loses something far greater than efficiency, it loses its *pulse*.

It stops being a place where ideas collide and becomes a place where they are managed. It stops producing breakthroughs and starts producing reports. It stops attracting dreamers and starts retaining caretakers.

That's the quiet end of innovation, not with layoffs or scandals, but with resignation. Not the kind you file with HR, but the kind you feel in your bones.

The human cost of bureaucracy is measured not in dollars or deadlines, but in potential never realized. It's in the engineer who once stayed late to perfect a design but now stays late to update a slide deck. It's in the scientist whose greatest discoveries live in notebooks, never approved for testing. It's in the leader who once inspired others to dare, now warning them to "manage expectations."

It's in the slow, unacknowledged loss of joy, the shift from *I get to* to *I have to.*

That's what bureaucracy steals in the end: not just innovation but meaning. It turns work from creation into maintenance, from expression into obligation. And while companies can survive that transformation, greatness cannot.

Because innovation doesn't come from process, it comes from people who care enough to break one. And when a company teaches its people not to care, not to risk, not to move, it doesn't matter how brilliant its past was. Its future has already been decided.

Conclusion: When Motion Becomes Memory

Bureaucracy doesn't begin as failure, it begins as success. Every rule was once a solution. Every process was once a shortcut. Every layer of oversight was once added for good reason. But over time, those reasons fade, and the systems that once enabled progress begin to preserve themselves instead.

The company that once lived in motion begins to live in memory. It remembers how it used to move, how it used to decide, how it used to feel when risk was a privilege, not a punishment. But memory cannot power innovation. It can only describe what was lost.

The death of speed rarely happens with drama. It happens quietly in meeting rooms and email threads, in the comfort of consensus and the illusion of order. No one kills innovation on purpose; they simply smother it with good intentions.

It happens every time a manager delays a decision "for alignment." Every time a committee rewrites an idea until it's safe. Every time an executive cancels a project because the numbers won't please investors next quarter. Each moment feels small, defensible, rational. But together, they create an organization that has learned to live without urgency.

And once a company loses urgency, it loses everything.

What follows is not collapse, but calcification. The company still moves, but mechanically, sustained by process, not purpose. Its people are still busy, but their work has lost tension, curiosity, and meaning. Its innovation department hosts workshops about agility while the real opportunities pass by unnoticed.

From the outside, it still looks successful: profitable, efficient, "well-managed." From the inside, it feels like slow suffocation, a culture where no one remembers what it's like to take a risk that matters.

This is bureaucracy's final form: a system designed to eliminate uncertainty that ends up eliminating possibility.

And yet, the story is not hopeless. Every organization carries within it the memory of speed, the DNA of its founding energy, the instinct to move. But to rediscover it requires more than process reform or motivational slogans. It requires a kind of corporate unlearning: the courage to dismantle what once made it strong. Some will never do it. They will grow quieter, safer, and eventually irrelevant. But a few will find the nerve to move again, to break their own systems before the market does it for them.

In the next chapter, we'll meet them. The ones who set the tempo, who decide whether fear or curiosity rules the room. Because behind every slow company is a cautious leader, and behind every innovative one is a leader who made movement inevitable.

PART 2

The Systemic Barriers to Innovation

Every company begins with the courage to try. It's what turns founders into builders and ideas into motion. But somewhere between the first spark and the first billion in revenue, that courage gets managed into compliance. The company stops asking *"what if?"* and starts asking *"what's the risk?"*

The truth is, most corporations don't run out of ideas, they run into systems. And those systems, built with good intentions, quietly train the organization to value predictability over possibility. They turn innovation from an instinct into an event.

These are the systemic barriers, invisible yet everywhere, that make even the brightest companies slow. They don't appear overnight. They evolve as success accumulates, as efficiency becomes doctrine, as growth becomes maintenance. Each barrier begins as protection and ends as paralysis.

Three forces, in particular, do the most damage:

1. Bureaucracy that suffocates speed. Layers multiply. Meetings metastasize. Every decision now requires a memo, a model, a meeting, and a sign-off. What began as process for safety becomes ritual for its own sake. The organization learns to wait instead of move, to report instead of act. The most creative people stop asking permission, they stop asking at all.

2. Financial gravity. The market's calendar becomes the company's conscience. Every ninety days, the question is not "what did we learn?" but "did we hit it?" Innovation that can't be forecasted on a spreadsheet is quietly sidelined. The tyranny of the quarter teaches leaders to think in increments, not leaps.

3. Cultural inertia. Success writes habits into muscle memory. The playbook that once built advantage becomes the script that no one dares to deviate from. Employees learn that it's safer to refine than to reinvent, safer to protect what works than to question why it does. The company's culture begins to orbit its own history.

None of this is intentional. Bureaucracy is born from scale, not malice. Financial caution is born from accountability, not cowardice. Cultural inertia is born from pride in what worked. But together, they form a perfect ecosystem for stagnation, a world where the cost of change feels greater than the cost of decay.

This part of the book pulls the curtain back on those forces. We'll follow how bureaucracy evolves from efficiency to suffocation, how Wall Street's rhythm reshapes corporate imagination, and how leadership habits harden into walls that block the very future they claim to build.

But this is not just an autopsy; it's reconnaissance. To dismantle what slows us, we must first see how it's built, the meetings that disguise fear as rigor, the dashboards that reward motion instead of progress, the leadership behaviors that measure alignment instead of learning.

Innovation doesn't die because of bad people or bad ideas. It dies because systems outgrow their soul.

Understanding those systems, seeing the architecture of resistance, is the first act of recovery. Because once you can name what's slowing you, you can start designing a company that moves again.

CHAPTER 3

The Leadership Trap: How Good Management Becomes Bad for Innovation

Every company begins with belief, belief that a few people can do what the industry giants said was impossible. At first, that belief is contagious. The founders are close enough to feel the hum of the prototype, close enough to argue over a circuit, a line of code, or a line of poetry that might define the brand. They move fast, not because they're reckless, but because the world hasn't yet told them to slow down.

Then success arrives. Growth brings distance. The founder who once built is now briefed. Meetings replace whiteboards; forecasts replace curiosity. The language changes, too, *targets*, *pipelines*, *deliverables*. Words that sound responsible but quietly signal that imagination is no longer the priority.

That's when leadership becomes the dividing line between companies that *stay alive* and those that only *stay open*.

It's easy to blame bureaucracy or structure for the loss of speed, but behind every process sits a person who chose it. Behind every delayed decision, a leader who hesitated. And behind every faltering innovation program, a culture that learned, often unconsciously, that safety matters more than discovery.

Leadership, not systems, sets the emotional temperature of a company. If leaders treat risk like infection, teams will mask their ideas. If they treat failure like betrayal, curiosity will wither. If they chase predictability at all costs, even success will start to feel like decline.

Great leadership does the opposite. It makes risk feel noble, makes learning feel like winning, and makes innovation feel not like an initiative, but like breathing.

This chapter is about that kind of leadership, not the kind that manages what exists, but the kind that makes what's next *inevitable*.

Leadership as the Operating System

Titles describe authority; behaviors create reality. The true measure of leadership isn't found in an org chart, it's written in the reflexes of the people below it. Every meeting, every decision, every silence teaches the organization what matters.

In every conversation, leaders are unconsciously programming the culture. They teach it how to think:

- What's our default tempo, wait or move?
- What's our appetite for ambiguity, clarify or explore?
- What happens to people who try and fail, are they sidelined or studied?

These small cues accumulate faster than any strategy document. They decide whether curiosity is a virtue or a liability, whether urgency feels empowering or dangerous. When leaders pause too long to protect themselves from mistakes, the entire organization learns to wait. When they celebrate neat slides over messy progress, teams learn that presentation matters more than momentum.

Over time, these lessons harden into muscle memory. You don't need a policy to slow a company down, only leaders who reward caution. Fear becomes efficient. The company begins to conserve its energy for self-protection rather than discovery.

A company's operating system, then, isn't code or process, it's the sum of these daily micro-decisions. In healthy systems, leaders model curiosity, speed, and intellectual honesty. They ask, *"What did we learn?"* before *"What went wrong?"* In struggling systems, leaders demand certainty, punish surprise, and call that "accountability."

Leadership defines rhythm. It decides how fast information moves and how truth travels. When leaders listen deeply and decide quickly, they create an internal tempo that multiplies confidence. When they hesitate, waiting for consensus, for more data, for perfect timing, they quietly drain momentum.

In that sense, leadership is less about authority and more about energy transfer. It's kinetic. A great leader doesn't simply approve motion, they generate it. They don't need to tell people to care; they behave in ways that make caring feel inevitable.

The healthiest organizations are led by people who understand that culture isn't declared, it's demonstrated. Their leadership operating system is built on three principles:

1. **Curiosity over certainty.** They reward questions that reveal blind spots, not answers that confirm assumptions.
2. **Speed over symmetry.** They'd rather fix a small mistake tomorrow than debate a perfect plan forever.
3. **Learning over blame.** They treat errors as prototypes of wisdom, not proof of incompetence.

When this mindset cascades downward, innovation doesn't need a department, it becomes instinct. People act without asking because the operating system has taught them that progress is safer than paralysis.

And when it doesn't? Meetings multiply, projects linger, and nobody remembers when the company last felt *alive*.

A Tale of Two Leaders

Picture two companies facing the same bad quarter.

Both missed forecasts. Both saw competitors launch faster. Both have teams exhausted from working hard and still feeling behind.

In the first company, the Monday meeting begins with tension so thick it feels physical. The CEO opens the call with metrics and disappointment: *"We cannot afford another miss."* Each leader defends their numbers, promising new controls, new sign-offs, new dashboards. By the end, everyone feels smaller but safer. The message is clear: move only when certain.

In the second company, the tone is completely different. The CEO opens with a question, not a reprimand: *"What did we learn that our competitors learned faster?"* The room exhales. People start talking, honestly this time. One admits a product delay wasn't technical but bureaucratic. Another confesses they've been chasing the wrong KPI. Instead of assigning blame, the CEO reframes the failure as data: *"Then we're paying tuition. Let's make the lesson worth the cost."*

The contrast couldn't be sharper. Both companies missed their target, but only one learned how to move again. In the first, leaders protected their egos. In the second, they protected their capacity to learn.

Six months later, the difference is visible on every floor. In the first company, hallways are quiet, inboxes careful, and decisions slow. In the second, prototypes move out faster than memos. Risk hasn't vanished, it's been domesticated. The culture no longer fears the unknown; it treats it as familiar terrain.

That is the power of leadership as an operating system. It doesn't need permission from HR, or an offsite, or a new initiative. It rewrites the company's instincts from the top down, one reaction at a time.

Leaders don't just steer organizations; they teach them how to feel. When the feeling is fear, even the smartest people play small. But when the feeling is trust, the organization moves like a living thing, fast, adaptable, alert, and alive.

The Science Beneath the Instinct

The patterns we call "culture" are really patterns of chemistry. Every time a leader reacts, with anger, curiosity, or calm, they trigger a biochemical response that either narrows or expands the organization's collective thinking. It's not metaphorical; it's physiological.

When leaders create fear, teams experience a surge of cortisol and adrenaline, chemicals that sharpen short-term focus but suppress exploration and creativity. The brain becomes excellent at survival, not invention. People think narrowly, seek safety in consensus, and hesitate to take risks that might draw criticism. In this mode, organizations operate like anxious bodies: hypervigilant, reactive, incapable of rest or play, two states where creativity actually flourishes.

Conversely, when leaders project trust and curiosity, they trigger a release of oxytocin and dopamine, the chemistry of connection and reward. These chemicals expand the brain's ability to associate, imagine, and take calculated risks. Teams in such environments literally think broader thoughts. They recover faster from setbacks because their emotional circuitry isn't trapped in defense. They collaborate more openly because their nervous systems no longer treat coworkers as threats.

This isn't soft science. Decades of research in organizational psychology and neuroscience, from Amy Edmondson's work on *psychological safety* to Daniel Kahneman's findings on *fast and slow thinking*, all point to the same conclusion: leadership behaviors alter the cognitive bandwidth of the people who follow. Tone sets tempo, and tempo determines whether an organization learns or stagnates.

That's why companies with visionary or adaptive leaders so often outperform their bureaucratic peers even with fewer resources. It's not just strategy; it's neurobiology. They've built an environment where the brain's most creative states, curiosity, flow, and intrinsic motivation, are not rare events but daily habits.

In the end, innovation isn't simply a process to manage. It's a state of mind to protect, and leaders are its primary architects.

From Instinct to Intent

The most effective leaders understand that emotion precedes execution. Before they ask for innovation, they design for it, not through slogans or incentives, but by shaping the psychological environment where innovation can survive. They treat morale as infrastructure and trust as capital.

The shift from instinct to intent marks the difference between ordinary management and transformative leadership. Ordinary leaders manage what people do. Transformative leaders manage what people *feel* while they do it.

And feelings, though invisible, dictate everything. A single sentence from a senior leader can either compress an entire department into silence or ignite it into motion. When leadership energy is steady, people take risks. When it wavers, people retreat. Culture, at its core, is the echo of leadership behavior.

That brings us to the archetypes, patterns of leadership energy that determine how organizations evolve. Each model creates a distinct rhythm, a distinct relationship with risk, and a distinct kind of company.

Four Leadership Archetypes (and What They Do to Innovation)

1) Visionary Leadership: Expansive Futures, Decisive Bets

Visionary leaders make the future feel tangible. They don't just describe what's coming, they *compress time*, allowing people to experience the next decade in the present moment. Their energy converts skepticism into conviction and hesitation into motion.

Steve Jobs did this at Apple. In 2007, he walked onstage holding what looked like an ordinary phone, but he spoke as though he were revealing civilization's next interface. "An iPod, a phone, an Internet communicator..." The room didn't just see a device, they saw an era opening. What made Jobs singular wasn't the product, but his ability to collapse engineering, art, and aspiration into one coherent vision. He was unreasonable in the literal sense of the word, his expectations defied the reasoning of his time. And in that defiance, he made the future contagious.

Reed Hastings of Netflix shares a different form of visionary courage, quieter, but equally transformative. When he decided to end the company's DVD-by-mail business, even his board thought he was premature. Streaming was clunky, broadband uneven, studios hostile. But Hastings bet on inevitability. "It's not a matter of *if* streaming replaces physical media," he said, "it's *when*, and whether we'll be the ones leading it." That sentence reframed fear as timing, not fate. Within five years, the move that once looked reckless became prophetic.

Visionary leaders operate with two rare convictions: that the present is temporary, and that the future can be built through story as much as through strategy. Their greatest tool isn't a plan, it's belief distribution.

- **Strengths:** Clarity, narrative energy, market creation.
- **Risks:** Blind spots, hero culture, underinvestment in systems.
- **When it works:** When the vision is paired with *frictionless execution* and leaders who prune aggressively.

Visionary leadership turns uncertainty into gravity. People stop asking for guarantees and start asking for roles. The best visionaries don't demand faith, they *earn it* through coherence, through the simple act of making the impossible sound like the next logical step.

2) Adaptive Leadership: *Direction with humility*

If visionary leaders make the future believable, adaptive leaders make it achievable. They know that bold ideas are meaningless without mechanisms that let people learn, adjust, and try again. Where visionaries expand possibility, adaptive leaders orchestrate evolution.

Their gift isn't certainty, it's composure in uncertainty. They move organizations forward not by insisting on being right, but by building systems that *learn fast enough to recover when wrong.*

Satya Nadella's transformation of Microsoft stands as one of the defining case studies of adaptive leadership in modern business. When he became CEO in 2014, Microsoft was still profitable but stagnant, trapped in internal rivalries, territorial silos, and an engineering culture addicted to winning debates instead of customers. Nadella didn't start with a reorg or a product announcement; he started with tone.

"Empathy," he said, "is the key to innovation." The word sounded dissonant inside a company long known for technical dominance and competitive aggression. But Nadella's empathy wasn't sentimental, it was strategic. He reframed it as intellectual humility, the foundation for curiosity and collaboration. Under his watch, teams that once fought over platforms began building shared ecosystems. Engineers who once dismissed open-source embraced it. Microsoft rediscovered its rhythm, not through conquest, but through connection.

Nadella's genius wasn't in predicting trends; it was in creating an environment flexible enough to meet them. He taught the company how to learn again, to stop asking, *"Are we right?"* and start asking, *"Are we learning fast enough?"*

A similar pattern defines Mary Barra's tenure at General Motors. When she took over in 2014, GM was burdened by bureaucracy, haunted by recalls, and culturally risk-averse Barra's challenge wasn't to make GM bigger, but to make it braver. She did what few automotive leaders dared: restructured legacy divisions, cut unprofitable lines, and invested heavily in electric and autonomous technologies years before the market was ready.

Her approach wasn't about chasing headlines but about changing habits. "We can't control the wind," she told her executives, "but we can build better sails." In a century-old company built for consistency, Barra injected the muscle memory of adaptation.

Both Nadella and Barra share the quiet courage that defines adaptive leadership, the ability to act decisively while holding the outcome lightly. They understand that leading through change is less about predicting the right future and more about designing an organization capable of thriving in *any* future.

- **Strengths:** Resilience, compounding insight, survivability in volatile markets.
- **Risks:** Perception of wavering if communication lags.
- **When it works:** When the *cadence* is defined (monthly/quarterly reviews), and pivots are framed as progress, not retreat.

Adaptive leadership thrives in complexity because it accepts complexity as the price of relevance. It transforms uncertainty from an enemy into an asset, and in doing so, it ensures that innovation isn't just possible, but sustainable.

3) Servant Leadership: *Unblocking at scale*

Servant leaders don't innovate *through* authority, they innovate *by releasing* it. They understand that creativity doesn't respond to orders; it responds to ownership. Their power comes not from directing people, but from removing the friction that keeps people from doing their best work.

The philosophy sounds simple, *leaders exist to serve their teams*, but in practice, it requires immense strength. It means surrendering ego, sharing credit, and trusting others enough to give them control. It means believing that leadership is less about being the smartest person in the room and more about ensuring everyone else can think freely.

Indra Nooyi embodied this kind of leadership at PepsiCo. When she became CEO in 2006, the company faced a paradox: it was profitable but misaligned with the growing cultural shift toward health and sustainability. The easy path would have been optimization, bigger marketing budgets, new flavors, and tighter cost control. But Nooyi saw further. She reframed PepsiCo's purpose around "Performance with Purpose", the idea that a global corporation could be financially successful *and* socially responsible.

This wasn't branding. It was structural. She invested billions into healthier product lines, reduced environmental impact, and championed employee wellness long before ESG became corporate vocabulary. Critics said she was diluting focus; investors doubted the returns. Yet her leadership didn't rest on command, it rested on conviction and inclusion. She asked teams to co-design the company's evolution. "If you want people to take ownership," she once said, "you must invite them into the mission."

Under her, PepsiCo became a learning organism, one that outperformed rivals not by chasing trends, but by nurturing trust and long-term purpose. Her kind of service wasn't passive; it was transformational. She didn't remove accountability, she made it collective.

Across the country, in a very different kind of business, Tony Hsieh of Zappos built his own brand of servant leadership, playful, radical, and human. Where Nooyi integrated empathy into a Fortune 500, Hsieh built a culture around it entirely. His belief was simple: happy employees make happy customers, and everything else follows.

At Zappos, titles mattered less than trust. Customer service reps were empowered to spend hours solving a single problem without scripts or approval limits. The company famously encouraged weirdness, conversation, and connection, what Hsieh called "creating a little more happiness in the world."

When other CEOs obsessed over metrics, Hsieh obsessed over *meaning*. He believed that freedom was a management strategy. "If you want your team to take care of customers," he said, "you have to take care of your team first." That idea, radical in its simplicity, turned Zappos from a struggling startup into one of the most beloved brands in retail.

Both Nooyi and Hsieh practiced servant leadership, but through different tones.

- Nooyi's was *architectural*, reshaping a global enterprise through inclusion and shared purpose.
- Hsieh's was *cultural*, proving that joy and freedom could scale profitability.

In both cases, they built companies that didn't just work, they *felt alive.*

- **Strengths:** Psychological safety, discretionary effort, durable trust.
- **Risks:** Drift into consensus if boundaries aren't clear.
- **When it works:** When empowerment is paired with crisp guardrails, clear strategy, budgets, and stage-gates.

Servant leadership may seem gentle, but it's one of the hardest forms of power. It requires the courage to lead from behind, to let others be visible, to measure success in the autonomy of others, and to build systems so strong they no longer depend on you.

4) Transactional Leadership: *Precision without possibility*

Transactional leaders are the caretakers of consistency. They ensure systems run, metrics are met, and surprises are eliminated. Their power lies in control, but so does their vulnerability.

They are invaluable in industries where reliability is non-negotiable: aerospace, finance, manufacturing. They thrive on order, predictability, and precision. But when markets shift or technology leaps forward, their instincts become liabilities. They optimize for yesterday's reality.

Consider IBM in the early 2010s. Once the symbol of disciplined excellence, it became a company managed almost entirely by spreadsheets. Under Ginni Rometty, the focus turned to quarterly predictability: share buybacks, head-count trimming, and incremental service contracts. The machine kept humming, but the imagination engine stalled. Innovation became an accounting line, not a belief. By the time cloud competitors like Amazon and

Microsoft redefined the landscape, IBM was still rearranging its dashboards. It wasn't a failure of intelligence, it was a failure of permission. Leaders rewarded efficiency, and efficiency quietly killed exploration.

A similar story unfolded at General Electric. GE had once been the gold standard of management discipline, but by the 2000s it became trapped in its own systems. Under successive transactional leaders, the company doubled down on financial optimization, divesting, merging, and repackaging divisions to please investors. The result was precision without purpose. GE could measure everything except momentum. When the world pivoted toward renewable energy and software-driven manufacturing, GE's reflexes were still tuned to margins, not reinvention.

Transactional leaders rarely intend to stifle innovation; they simply trust measurement more than imagination. In calm markets, this works brilliantly. In turbulent ones, it breeds paralysis. Their obsession with control becomes a tax on curiosity.

- **Strengths:** Reliability, cost discipline, operational excellence.
- **Risks:** Innovation theater, sanded-down ideas, talent flight.
- **When it works:** As a *mode*, not a religion, used to scale what's proven, not to discover what's next.

Transactional leadership isn't wrong, it's incomplete. It keeps organizations stable long enough to survive disruption, but not flexible enough to create it. The best leaders know when to toggle this mode on and when to let it go. Because innovation requires moments of productive chaos, and no spreadsheet in history has ever forecasted a breakthrough.

The Leadership Trap: When Strength Becomes Stagnation

Every leadership style carries within it the seed of its own undoing. What begins as a strength, focus, control, empathy, discipline, can quietly mutate into a barrier. The same instincts that build enduring companies can also make them resistant to change.

Visionary leaders, for instance, can become prisoners of their own clarity. The future they once saw so vividly hardens into doctrine. Teams stop questioning the vision and start performing it by rote. Dissent feels like disloyalty. What was once bold becomes brittle. History is full of leaders who confused conviction with omniscience, who mistook yesterday's breakthrough for tomorrow's truth.

Adaptive leaders, in contrast, can fall into *perpetual adjustment mode*. Their humility and openness, essential for learning, can slide into indecision. When every path is provisional and every choice revisited, momentum dissolves. The organization becomes a reflection loop, smart, aware, and endlessly hesitant.

Servant leaders risk a subtler trap: the culture of comfort. When empathy outpaces accountability, urgency erodes. The organization grows kind but slow, high in trust, low in tension. People feel safe, but not stretched. Without the productive discomfort that innovation demands, psychological safety turns into complacency.

And transactional leaders, the masters of process, often mistake activity for progress. Their pursuit of precision becomes a pursuit of permanence. They sand down every rough edge until the organization is frictionless, and lifeless. Innovation suffocates under the weight of consistency.

These are not moral failings; they're gravitational forces. Every leader faces the pull toward safety, the comfort of predictability, the ease of control, the serenity of consensus. But innovation lives in disequilibrium. It requires friction, contradiction, and sometimes chaos.

Leadership becomes a hindrance to innovation when it over-optimizes for stability. When clarity becomes rigidity, humility becomes hesitation, empathy becomes avoidance, and control becomes fear.

The paradox is simple and devastating: the very behaviors that made a company great can make it obsolete.

The organizations that stagnate are rarely led by the incompetent. They're led by the consistent, people who did what once worked, long after the world had moved on.

The Hidden Killers: Four Failure Modes of Leadership

Innovation doesn't usually die from incompetence. It dies quietly, from behaviors that look responsible, rational, even wise. The great irony is that these failure modes are celebrated inside boardrooms. They wear the costume of discipline. They sound like good management. And that's what makes them so lethal.

1. Fear Masquerading as Rigor

Some of the most cautious organizations in the world believe they are being careful, when in truth, they are simply afraid. Meetings multiply. Risk reviews expand. The word alignment becomes a shield for indecision. Everyone agrees to "wait for more data," yet no one counts the opportunity cost of delay. Over time, rigor becomes ritual, a performance of seriousness that hides a paralysis of spirit.

True rigor asks hard questions and acts on the answers. False rigor just asks the same questions again until the moment to act has passed. The fear of being wrong quietly outweighs the desire to be right. Innovation suffocates under the paperwork of prudence.

2. Vanity Metrics

What gets measured gets managed, and what gets managed eventually gets gamed. Dashboards fill with numbers that signal progress but not impact: patents filed instead of products shipped, prototypes demoed instead of customers delighted. Teams learn to play to the scoreboard rather than the marketplace.

Vanity metrics offer comfort without insight. They create a sense of momentum while disguising stagnation. A company can appear busy, even heroic, while going nowhere. It's activity theater dressed as achievement.

The antidote is brutal honesty. Ask not "How much did we do?" but "What changed because we did it?" In that small shift of language lies the difference between motion and movement.

3. Certainty Addiction

Innovation lives in probability; bureaucracy craves proof. When leaders demand guarantees before greenlighting a new idea, they unknowingly reward only the safe and the obvious. Entire divisions learn that it's better to be confidently wrong than uncertainly right. The organization becomes allergic to ambiguity, and therefore to discovery.

Certainty feels like control, but it's often just ignorance with a clean spreadsheet. Great companies learn to trade perfection for momentum. They move while the data is incomplete, trusting iteration over prediction. Because in fast-changing industries, the cost of hesitation almost always exceeds the cost of error.

4. Distance

The final killer is distance, the slow drift between those who decide and those who do. As organizations grow, leaders ascend into abstraction. They manage symbols instead of experiences: charts, slide decks, and quarterly summaries that flatten the world into averages. But innovation never happens in the averages; it happens at the edges, where users complain, engineers tinker, and the future first whispers its intent.

When leaders stop visiting those edges, they lose the ability to feel reality. They manage the illusion of progress, not the substance of it. The PowerPoint becomes the product. The boardroom becomes the echo chamber.

The cure isn't heroic. It's habitual. Great leaders institutionalize dissent, reward honesty, and seek friction before it finds them. They walk factory floors, sit with customers, and ask questions that shrink the distance between title and truth:

- *What would we do if we were smaller?*
- *What did we learn this week that changed our mind?*

These questions seem simple, but they're acts of rebellion against the inertia of success. They remind everyone, including the leader, that growth without curiosity is just repetition with better furniture.

The Quiet Cost of Leadership Drift

When companies slow down, the world rarely notices right away. Revenue still arrives, meetings still happen, and plans still look polished. But beneath the surface, leadership drift begins, the quiet shift from exploring to defending, from learning to explaining, from doing to reviewing. Fear, vanity, certainty, and distance are just symptoms of that drift.

These are not external constraints; they're internal defaults. They emerge when leaders mistake management for momentum, or process for progress. Over time, the culture learns the lesson: *play it safe, look busy, never be wrong.* The organization doesn't collapse, it calcifies.

Innovation doesn't die in one moment of failure. It dies in the thousand unmade decisions that were waiting for permission. And that permission almost always flows from the top.

This is the hidden cost of success: the very systems designed to scale excellence begin to regulate imagination. Leadership, the operating system of the enterprise, becomes infected with its own defenses.

In the next chapter, we'll explore how this internal caution is often reinforced, and rewarded, by external forces. Shareholders, analysts, and financial markets demand predictability from companies that were built on disruption. The result is a dangerous alignment: leaders who fear volatility and investors who punish it. Together, they form the ultimate innovation paradox, the corporation that fears its own growth.

Diagnosing the Drift

Most companies don't wake up one morning to find they've lost their edge. It happens slowly, hidden under the weight of good intentions and polished plans. Processes become a comfort blanket. Data becomes a shield. Leaders start managing the illusion of control instead of the reality of progress.

The only reliable way to spot this decay is through questions that make people uncomfortable, questions that reveal not what the company *does*, but how it *thinks*. These are not metrics; they're mirrors. When answered honestly, they expose the reflexes that silently turn agility into ritual, creativity into compliance, and leadership into maintenance.

The following ten questions are not meant to diagnose individuals but systems, to uncover the subtle ways leadership behavior, structure, and culture conspire to slow innovation. Every organization that has lost its inventive spirit can trace the cause to one or more of these patterns.

1. **When was the last time we made a decision without a slide deck?** If the answer is "no one remembers," bureaucracy has replaced judgment. Leaders are performing confidence, not practicing it.
2. **What's harder in our company right now, getting a good idea or getting approval for it?** If the second takes longer, innovation isn't the problem. Governance is.
3. **Do people bring bad news early, or only when it's defensible?** When honesty requires evidence, truth arrives too late. Fear has entered the system.
4. **How often do we kill projects for being wrong versus for being late?** If timeliness matters more than learning, speed has become cosmetic. The clock is running, but progress isn't.
5. **When was the last time a frontline employee changed our mind?** If the hierarchy no longer transmits insight upward, leadership is managing in a vacuum. Distance is masquerading as perspective.

6. **What's celebrated more, outcomes or optics?** If dashboards look good but customers don't notice, the company is managing perception, not performance.

7. **What percentage of our meetings create new decisions rather than defend old ones?** If the number is low, the leadership culture has drifted from curiosity to control.

8. **How much of our talent's time is spent explaining their work instead of advancing it?** Excessive reporting is the scar tissue of mistrust. It signals a company that confuses visibility with accountability.

9. **When we say "risk," do we mean financial, reputational, or emotional?** Most organizations only manage the first two, and ignore the third. But emotional risk is where creativity actually lives.

10. **If we were half our size, what would we do differently tomorrow?** This is the litmus test of agility. If the answer includes "move faster" or "decide quicker," bureaucracy, not scale, is the true constraint.

Reading the Answers

The danger isn't in answering "wrong." The danger is answering *smoothly*. Healthy organizations debate these questions openly. Stagnant ones recite polished responses that hide discomfort. Innovation returns the moment leaders rediscover the humility to ask, *"What if the problem isn't our market, it's our management?"*

Answering these questions isn't an exercise in management hygiene, it's an act of organizational courage. The goal isn't to assign blame but to reveal where belief has turned into bureaucracy. Every mature company eventually builds structures to protect what it has built. Over time, those structures begin to protect themselves.

The tragedy is that no one notices when it happens. The slides still look convincing. The mission statements still sound inspiring. But the pulse changes. Meetings grow heavier, curiosity grows quieter, and the most talented people begin to withdraw. What disappears first isn't innovation, it's *permission*. Permission to ask, to experiment, to be wrong in pursuit of what might be right.

These ten questions help leaders find that pulse again. They are a mirror held up not to performance, but to posture, how an organization stands when confronted with uncertainty. Do we lean in or lean back? Do we explore or explain? Do we protect the system or the spark that built it?

True renewal begins not with a new initiative or vision statement, but with awareness, the simple acknowledgment that the barriers to innovation are not out there in the market, but in here, in the habits and reflexes of leadership itself.

Because in the end, innovation doesn't depend on size, budget, or even talent. It depends on the courage to see what comfort has made invisible, and to lead differently once you do.

Conclusion: When Leadership Becomes Management

Leadership is the most underestimated variable in innovation. We tend to attribute creative success to resources, technology, or timing, but more often, it begins and ends with tone. A single leader's instincts about speed, risk, and control can shape an entire organization's relationship with the unknown.

Every company develops habits from its leaders. The way they react to failure, the questions they ask, the permission they grant, these form the invisible architecture beneath all strategy. When that architecture rewards caution, the culture learns to hide curiosity.

When it rewards image, truth withers. When it rewards control, initiative dies.

Great leadership is not about charisma or vision alone. It's about maintaining the organization's emotional range, its ability to stay curious under pressure, fast under scrutiny, and united under doubt. The strongest leaders are those who preserve movement when everything else demands stillness.

But most companies don't lose innovation through neglect, they lose it through success. As growth compounds, leaders slowly trade imagination for insurance. They overcorrect for volatility, systematize everything, and confuse consistency with competence. The result is a culture that prizes what is measurable over what is meaningful.

And yet, the story doesn't end there. Even when internal caution takes hold, it is often amplified, and justified, by forces outside the organization. Boards, analysts, and investors start demanding predictability from the very companies that once thrived on risk. Leadership behaviors that once slowed innovation become institutionalized by shareholder expectations.

In the next chapter, we'll examine this external dimension, how markets, boards, and quarterly pressures conspire to make short-term thinking appear rational. We'll see how Wall Street's appetite for certainty not only reshapes leadership behavior but systematically punishes long-term innovation.

Because in the modern corporation, the most dangerous enemy of innovation is not incompetence, it's success managed for the wrong audience.

CHAPTER 4

The Shareholder Dilemma

The Quarter That Ate the Decade

Every enduring company begins as a wager on time. Its founders bet that patience will outlast panic, that the value of ideas, people, and learning compounds faster than short-term metrics can measure. They hire for potential, not polish. They fund experiments that may look wasteful today but inevitable tomorrow. They accept ambiguity because invention never unfolds on schedule. This is how institutions are born, not from efficiency, but from endurance.

Then time itself changes meaning. The rhythm of building, once measured in cycles of learning and iteration, is replaced by the rhythm of accounting. The calendar no longer tracks progress, it tracks pressure. What was once a horizon becomes a deadline. The slow art of compounding gives way to the fast theater of performance.

And then the calendar takes the throne. Not the calendar of craft, the one that measures field tests, prototypes, and capability built through repetition, but the calendar of finance. It tolls every ninety days with a single, blunt question: *Did you hit it?* The work of years is compressed into a line read aloud in a fluorescent room. The nuance of building becomes footnotes and Q&A. The company learns to breathe on a metronome that was never designed for invention.

Earnings day is a ritual of compression. In the morning, engineers wrestle with stubborn physics. By afternoon, those struggles must be translated into guidance. By evening, the market has delivered its verdict on a story that is still being written. If the number is clean, the stock smiles and everyone relaxes into the illusion that progress and predictability are the same thing. If it isn't, the company is punished, not for being wrong, but for being real.

What happens next is quiet. No alarms, no overhaul, just a series of sensible adjustments that feel like stewardship and add up to surrender.

The first adjustment is semantic. Vision becomes "visibility." Risk becomes "prudence." Investment becomes "expense." Leaders stop saying what they will build and start saying what they will not surprise. Language doesn't merely describe reality; it edits it. Inside the new dictionary, the safest sentence in the company is, "Let's push that to next quarter."

The second adjustment is calendrical. Launches slip "for sequencing." Gate reviews migrate to the bright side of quarters so they are easier to narrate. Pilots are timed for investor days rather than user need. Work begins to orbit the call. It is still good work, but gravity has changed.

The third adjustment is arithmetic. The projects with ambiguous timelines, platforms, architectures, step-change cost curves, start losing arguments to projects that polish what already exists. It is easy to justify a marketing tranche that moves a number next month; it is hard to defend a materials program that moves physics next year. The budget flows to the immediate because immediacy is measurable.

Over time, these adjustments become doctrine. The company doesn't decide to be short-term. It becomes short-term by being careful.

There are three invisible taxes the quarter charges on the decade:

1. **The Optionality Tax.** Every time you defer a platform in favor of a feature, you pay with options you will not have later. Options do not appear on financial statements, but they decide who sets prices in five years.
2. **The Learning Attrition.** Experiments that would have failed fast and taught you something are never run. The team looks tidy. The roadmap looks plausible. The knowledge base stops growing at the edges, the only place that matters.
3. **The Calendar Drift.** The internal calendar and the external one quietly decouple. Customers evolve on their own time. Regulators move on theirs. Competitors ship on theirs. Only your company believes reality should respect a fiscal quarter.

This drift is not theoretical. It has a texture you can feel.

You see it when a hardware team freezes a design that needs another pass because the slip would push recognition into next year, and "next year" is no one's bonus. You see it when a software org ships a "minimum lovable product" that is minimum and not lovable, because love is hard to measure on a Thursday afternoon. You see it when supply chain approvals are held to protect gross margin on a call, only to pay twice as much later when the world refuses to read your script.

The most corrosive effect is cultural. The quarter trains people where courage belongs. Not in the lab, where it costs money; in the deck, where it costs adjectives. The company starts to attract and reward the kind of intelligence that can *explain* anything and *change* very little. Careers are built on smoothing volatility, not harnessing it. Smart people become expert handlers of surprise rather than makers of it.

Anatomy of a miss:

- **Quarter -2:** A team proposes a risky subsystem that halves unit cost at scale. Leadership is supportive, but the current quarter looks tight.
- **Quarter -1:** Procurement flags variance. Finance suggests an "orderly phase-in" after year-end. Everyone agrees, because everyone is reasonable.
- **Quarter 0:** The company hits the number. Press applauds discipline. The subsystem is re-scoped as a "multi-phase exploration."
- **Quarter +2:** A competitor ships the cost curve you chose not to. Your number is still fine. Your future is not.

No memo announces this erosion. The graphs look beautiful until they don't. That is the danger of clean lines: they cannot show what is rotting under the paint.

Leaders sometimes respond by asking for "innovation within the quarter." That phrase sounds motivating; it is impossible. Breakthroughs respect cycles of discovery, synthesis, and iteration that do not fit neatly between earnings calls. When you force the work to present itself on a rhythm it does not obey, you do not accelerate it, you counterfeit it. Demos replace prototypes. Pilots replace products. Narratives replace learning.

The alternative is harder at first and cheaper forever: tell the truth about time and structure the company to live inside that truth.

- **Make the long arc legible.** Report the health of capability with the same rigor as revenue: cost curves, reliability curves, adoption curves, learning cycle time. Teach investors what progress actually looks like before you need their patience.

- **Protect the messy middle.** Create budgets and guardrails that cannot be raided to "make the quarter." If a program is strategic, make it unkillable for cosmetic reasons. If it is not, have the courage to kill it loudly and early.

- **Reward slope, not intercept.** Compensate leaders for the rate of improvement in things that compound, unit economics, cycle times, quality, share, over multi-year windows. Let grants vest on the timescale of moats, not media cycles.

- **Rehearse volatility.** Normalize misses in service of step-changes. If your organization has never explained an ugly quarter with a beautiful rationale, it is not investing hard enough.

The discipline here is not austerity; it is sequence. Spend lavishly where learning accelerates and ruthlessly where it doesn't. Ship prototypes that embarrass you slightly. Accept that the call may not like it. The call is not your customer.

There is a simple test to know whether the quarter is eating your decade: ask five leaders, separately, what they would do differently if there were no earnings call for four quarters. If their answers are bolder than your plan, you are negotiating with a calendar instead of building a company.

The truth, inconvenient and liberating, is this: markets will forgive volatility in service of inevitability. They will not forgive smoothness in service of decay. You cannot charm a decade. You can only earn it, one unglamorous cycle at a time, by choosing experiments over optics, capability over cosmetics, and the slow, compounding discipline of work that may not read well on a transcript but will be obvious in hindsight.

That is the real job of leadership under the tyranny of the short term: to miss neatly when you must, to explain honestly when you do, and to buy time, again and again, for the parts of the company that only time can build.

When Optics Replace Outcomes

Short-termism doesn't just change where money goes; it changes what courage looks like. Inside the walls, the scoreboard drifts from capability to appearance. The work keeps moving, but the meaning of "progress" shifts by a few quiet degrees until the graphs are green and the product is gray.

It starts with metric laundering. Numbers designed to inform begin to perform. A defect becomes a "variance." A delay becomes "re-sequencing." A pilot that taught nothing becomes a "learning milestone." Dashboards improve because definitions did, not because users did.

Then comes launch theater. Calendars determine truth. Announcements are choreographed for maximum narrative and minimum uncertainty: press, demo, applause, followed by weeks of retrofitting reality to match the slide. Adoption lags, but impressions look terrific.

Finally, stage-gate ritual replaces inquiry. Reviews ask, "Are we on plan?" rather than, "Are we getting better?" Evidence is curated to pass gates; experiments are scoped to succeed. Unknowns are renamed "TBDs" and scheduled into comfort.

You can feel this culture in small signatures:

- The best engineers are now the best slide authors.
- "Green" status travels faster than root-cause.
- Postmortems explain *surprises* more than they explain *physics*.
- Product health is narrated as sentiment (brand, buzz) rather than behavior (retention, reliability, unit cost).
- The path to "on-time" runs through revised definitions, not improved systems.

None of this requires cynicism, only incentives. People optimize what is visible. If visibility rewards tidiness, the organization will get tidier. If visibility rewards capability, the organization will get better.

The antidote is not rejecting metrics; it's re-privileging evidence:

- **Make capability legible.** Track learning velocity, time-to-root-cause, reliability curves, unit economics per build. Keep these unspinnable and mandatory in reviews.

- **Define "launch" as usage.** A feature isn't "done" until adoption crosses a threshold you'd be embarrassed to publish. Count behavior, not buzz.

- **Guard real experiments.** Fund tests that can *fail informatively*, not just *pass cosmetically*. Gates are passed by what we learned, not by how clean the deck reads.

- **Pay for slope.** Reward multi-quarter improvement in the things that compound, cost, quality, cycle time, retention, over slide-friendly wins.

- **Promote candor.** Public credit for early bad news; consequences for concealment. Make truth the safest political position in the room.

Optics are comfortable because they're fast and neat. Outcomes are costly because they're slow and specific. But only one of them compounds. Stories can sustain a quarter. Systems sustain a decade.

The EPS Religion

EPS is the cleanest lie in business. Change the denominator and call it progress. Nothing appears to move faster than a company that decides to count less of itself.

This is the quiet conversion that happens in large corporations. Earnings per share becomes scripture, buybacks the sacrament, and the quarterly call a kind of liturgy where executives testify to the purity of their discipline. The ritual is soothing: announce an authorization, execute in blackouts and windows, lift EPS, reassure the street that capital returned is capital respected. Applause follows. The graph listens.

Buybacks are not evil. They are a tool. But tools become religions when they replace judgment. In the EPS faith, the first commandment is neatness. Cash unused is a sin. Variance is a vice. Investment that cannot be forecast to the penny is heresy. The balance sheet looks stronger; the company becomes smaller.

It doesn't start with greed. It starts with a sentence that sounds responsible: *We're returning excess capital.* The sentence hides the only question that matters: excess relative to what? Relative to the next feature? Perhaps. Relative to the next platform, the next cost curve, the next factory, the next science bet that takes five years to look obvious? Almost never.

Denominator Management

It starts as arithmetic and ends as culture. Someone points at a simple truth: *per-share* numbers move if the share count moves. Revenue is hard. Margin is harder. EPS can be made cooperative. You don't have to change what the business does; you can change how many slices you cut it into. The room nods because the math is clean. Clean math becomes a habit.

The mechanics are crisp. Authorize a buyback. Pace it to the quarter. Front-load with an ASR so the EPS lift appears now while the broker finishes in the background. Message it as "returning excess capital." Layer in a repurchase "to offset dilution" from equity comp so the share count doesn't drift the wrong way. On paper, nothing dramatic happened; in practice, you shifted the center of gravity from building numerators to managing denominators.

Once adopted, the math teaches behavior. Budgets that once argued for capability start arguing for accretion. Forecast reviews spend more time on weighted-average shares outstanding than on unit cost curves. Guidance prep includes a slide called "share count bridge," which quietly outranks the slide about reliability. Per-share optics metastasize not just EPS, but FCF per share, revenue per share, "cash return per share." The company becomes a master of ratios that rise when slices shrink.

Calendars learn the trick. ASRs are timed to pair with "beat and raise" quarters; open-market buys fill in softer ones. Equity grants get nudged to windows where treasury-stock math is kindest. Announcements you fear will wobble the stock are scheduled after big repurchases have set a floor. Blackouts, originally a governance tool, become a throttle for how much denominator smoothing you can do in a given period. The stock's calendar starts editing the product's.

Accounting helps the illusion along without breaking a rule. GAAP carries the expense for share-based pay; non-GAAP invites it back out. The buyback, which converts that paper expense into cash spent, lives on the cash-flow statement far from the EPS slide that celebrates neatness. The audience hears one story, alignment and discipline, while the balance sheet quietly pays for both.

Denominator management also chooses your M&A. Accretive bolt-ons that add tidy per-share arithmetic outrank messy platform acquisitions that would consume cash and add shares (or debt) before they add advantage. Integration teams get very good at making dashboards glow green: Day-0 comms, Day-30 domain cutovers, Day-60 system merges. None of those dashboards measure the only line that matters, *did the platform's slope change?*, but the EPS column moved, so the deal is declared wise.

You can spot the culture by its reflexes. In reviews, someone asks, "What's the EPS impact?" before anyone asks, "What's the customer impact?" Finance wins arguments by bringing a denominator slide. Product learns to pre-phase proposals so the costly part that bends the curve lives just beyond the guidance horizon. Operations trims buffers because working capital tied up in inventory doesn't help per-share optics this quarter. Supply risk hides in the places per-share metrics don't look.

The final tell is the language. "Excess capital" appears in sentences that never define *excess relative to what timescale*. "Offsetting dilution" is used like a moral good, as if the goal of compensation were to be invisible rather than effective. "Accretion" becomes a synonym for wisdom. Each word files down an edge until progress itself is judged by how elegantly you can divide a number.

In the short run, denominator management feels like competence. The line goes up on schedule; the street applauds your "discipline." In the long run, it replaces the question *How big can the business become?* with *How small can the denominator be?* Numerators, customers, capability, cost curves, reliability, take longer to build and are harder to narrate. But they're the only parts that compound. The rest is arithmetic dressed as strategy.

The Three Myths of Buybacks

Myth 1: **"Buybacks prove we're undervalued."** This sounds decisive: if the stock is cheap, the smartest investment is ourselves. But "cheap" is a story from inside the building. Markets discount uncertainty about capability, your next platform, cost curve, and learning rate, not your confidence. Repurchases convert doubt into arithmetic without resolving the doubt. The price may lift; the reasons it sagged remain.

Myth 2: **"We have no better use for the cash."** What this really means is: we have no *certain* use for the cash. The projects that change slope, new architectures, supply-chain depth, automation, new routes to market, rarely satisfy certainty within a quarter. Cash gravitates to the path with the least rebuttal: the broker's window. "No better use" says more about an organization's tolerance for ambiguity than about the opportunity set.

Myth 3: **"Buybacks don't trade off with R&D."** Capital is rationed, in dollars and psychology. Celebrate repurchases loudly enough and every proposal is silently asked to beat the IRR of buying your own stock. Step-change bets lose to that bar on day one. Over time, the ritual rewires debate: questions about capability become questions about accretion.

Example: American Airlines' Pre-Crisis Neatness

In the mid-to-late 2010s, American Airlines found a storyline Wall Street loved: tidy EPS, confident guidance, and a steady cadence of repurchases that turned volatile operations into smooth per-share arithmetic. The logic was simple and persuasive on slides, strong demand, disciplined capacity growth, unit revenue holding, so "excess" cash could be returned. The applause was immediate; the trade-offs were not.

Inside the airline, those trade-offs had texture. Liquidity buffers stayed thin because cash on the balance sheet reads like "idle" capital in a quarterly script. Spare parts pools were optimized for averages, not shocks. Crew reserves were run lean, because coverage you don't use looks like waste. Irregular-operations playbooks, de-icing capacity, spare aircraft positioning, recovery gates, were staffed for most days, not bad weeks. None of this is reckless in isolation; all of it is fragile in combination.

Fleet strategy added another layer. American was midstream on a sweeping modernization, retiring older types and taking large batches of new narrowbodies and long-hauls. On paper, the plan promised fuel and maintenance savings; in practice, it concentrated deliveries and created rigidity. Lease returns, pilot qualifications, and line maintenance were scheduled like clockwork, great when the clock cooperates, unforgiving when it doesn't. The more fixed commitments you carry, the less room you have to absorb a hit without selling time, product, or both.

Under the surface, the capital structure began to make decisions for the operation. With repurchases celebrated, debt and fixed obligations quietly climbed. That reshaped debates: do you thicken the storm-recovery budget or beat the quarter? Do you over-provision spares for rare failures or keep DPO immaculate? Do you invest in baggage and crew-tracking systems that pay back in fewer meltdowns next year, or keep the EPS line neat this year? The spreadsheet wins those arguments because its benefits are certain and soon; resilience is uncertain and later.

When the shock arrived, the sudden collapse in demand, neatness evaporated. Liquidity that looked "disciplined" proved insufficient for zero-revenue weeks. The airline had to source emergency cash, restructure schedules at a scale playbooks weren't built for, and accept government support while pausing buybacks. The narrative flipped from "efficient capital return" to "survival," revealing how much of the prior strength was presentation, not posture. The lesson wasn't that modernization or capital return was inherently wrong; it's that years of optimizing to per-share optics crowds out the slow, unphotogenic investments, buffers, redundancies, systems, that turn an operator into a survivor.

What the Religion Rewires

EPS worship doesn't announce itself; it drifts in until the company keeps time to the transcript. Calendars outrank roadmaps; launches pivot to earnings week; windows and blackouts quietly set the tempo of truth. Progress is recast from product capability to deck-friendly certainty: green slides matter more than adoption. Capital debates favor what's legible and accretive now; step-changes are "phased" into disappearance. Reviews curate evidence to pass gates, not to learn. Language sands edges, expense becomes "efficiency," delay becomes "re-sequencing," dilution becomes "offset." Talent sorts: builders who bend cost curves drift out; narrators who smooth volatility drift up. Information follows the stock's calendar, bad news waits, good news blooms. Operations thin to flatter optics: stretched payables, shrinking buffers, hidden single-points. The center of gravity tilts until the one product everyone knows how to ship is the transcript itself, impeccable, punctual, and increasingly detached from the messy work the customer touches.

The result is a quiet reprogramming of judgment. Decisions optimize for *narratability*, what can be proven in a window, rather than for *durability*, what will compound over cycles. Risk is defined as variance on a call, not vulnerability in a system. Metrics become décor, postmortems become PR, and the organization grows excellent at preventing surprises while steadily forfeiting advantage. By the time the effects are visible outside, the inside has already learned a new instinct: protect the quarter, postpone the future.

You can diagnose EPS religion without opening a 10-K:

- The capital allocation slide is the most polished in the deck.
- Strategic updates culminate in authorization sizes, not capability milestones.
- "Optionality" appears only in M&A, never in internal platforms.
- Executives describe the stock as "our best investment." (It almost never is. If it were, your day job would be raising a fund.)

- The company treats dividends as old-fashioned but buybacks as modern, as if returning capital were innovation with better branding.

The Opportunity Cost That Never Prints

It never shows up as a line item. There is no account for *the thing we didn't build* or *the curve we didn't bend*. Opportunity cost is the quiet ledger that accrues off the books, written in the products you almost made and the customers you almost kept.

It starts in a room where the numbers look reasonable. A team brings in a plan, ugly at first glance, beautiful if you squint far enough. A new architecture that would halve unit cost after a messy, expensive year. A reliability overhaul that would lift retention by points that don't fit in a press release. The graphs have elbows instead of straight lines. Finance asks sensible questions. Can we phase it? Can we slip it? Can we do the safe half now and the dangerous half later? The room votes for prudence. No one feels like they killed anything. They just moved it.

Down the hall, a different decision lands gentler. Marketing gets another tranche for "lift." It will move a number next month. Sales gets enablement. It will move a number this quarter. The roadmap tilts a few degrees toward the visible. No alarms ring because nothing broke. The company is still moving. Movement can look like progress when the calendar does the grading.

In the lab, the cost of that vote is physical. A subsystem that should have been refactored is patched again. The patch works until it doesn't. The defect curve refuses to bend; support tickets multiply in quiet stacks. The team learns to ship around the pain. Quality feels like an attitude problem instead of a funded problem. Pride steps aside for compliance. No one puts that in a deck.

In operations, the cost looks like thinness. Buffers trimmed last year to make room for "returns" don't grow back. Single-source vendors become single points of failure. Lead times stretch. The supply chain runs tighter and faster, until it doesn't. When a component slips, the story on the call is "macro." Inside, everyone knows it was *micro*, a dependency that could have been diversified if anyone had budgeted for resilience that didn't glow on the dashboard.

In hiring, the cost sounds like hallway conversations. A staff engineer says they'll try one more cycle, then shrugs. The kind of person who bends physics doesn't argue long with a calendar. They leave without a farewell tour, join a company where courage is liquid, and ship the idea you almost did. HR calls it regrettable attrition, as if regret were a metric. The next quarter looks fine. The next decade won't.

At the customer, the cost is a feeling. The product they loved stops getting better in the ways that matter and starts getting better in the ways that show. More announcements, fewer improvements. More themes, fewer fixes. They don't cancel dramatically. They drift. Your pipeline stays full because pipelines always do, until the day it doesn't convert like it used to and the word "churn" becomes a character in leadership meetings.

The ghost ledger grows in the places slides don't measure: the weekend your team didn't spend making the prototype because the demo was already good enough for the keynote; the bet you split into phases that never reached the phase where it stopped being a bet and started being an advantage; the integration you skipped because the quarter was full; the test you didn't run because failure would have been inconvenient to narrate.

Occasionally the bill tries to make itself seen. A competitor ships a platform that makes your roadmap look like a list of adjectives. A cost curve drops on their side of the fence. Their retention does not spike; it thickens, quietly, like trust. You tell yourself they were lucky, or reckless, or subsidized by a hype cycle you refuse to join. Maybe. Or maybe they funded the same ugly year you deferred, and now they are cashing dividends your model doesn't know how to pronounce.

Accounting helps the illusion. Financial statements are rigorous about what happened and indifferent to what might have. They capture the price of an asset and the cost of a mistake; they do not capture the price of patience or the cost of delay. There's no footnote for the feature you chose not to harden, the factory you chose not to build, the redundancy you chose not to buy. You can run immaculate quarters on paper while surrendering territory in reality. The surrender doesn't appear until reality has finished taking it.

There is a meeting, some year later, where the conversation turns sincere. The charts stop working. Guidance can't be massaged into obedience. Someone asks the right question, *When did we fall behind?* and the answer isn't dramatic. It's a timestamp on a calendar no one saved: the day the risky subsystem became a phase; the day the platform became a pilot; the day the learning budget became a line you moved with good intentions.

Opportunity cost doesn't knock. It collects. It writes itself into the slope of your unit economics, the patience of your customers, the talent density on your hardest problems. It speaks last and only in totals. And when it finally appears, it does not ask for back pay. It reminds you that compounding waits for no one, least of all a company that mistook motion for progress and neatness for nerve.

Debt as Disguise

Leverage makes discipline look like courage. In a low-rate world, debt turns hesitation into action and action into EPS. The math is frictionless: borrow cheaply, retire shares, lift the denominator, declare "efficiency." Nothing in the product changes; everything in the transcript does. Cheap money gives executives the feeling of decisiveness without the burden of building.

Debt works because it hides in the right places. Interest drips into the income statement slowly; principal maturity lives in a footnote; covenants sit inside a document almost no one reads. Meanwhile, the buyback is immediate, photogenic, and numerically tidy. The reward is public. The risk is deferred. The deferral is the point.

The choreography is always the same. A revolver is upsized. Bonds are floated, some fixed, some floating, some convertible to sweeten the coupon. An accelerated share repurchase (ASR) prints an instant EPS lift. Guidance is reiterated. The chart cooperates. Headlines say "confidence." Inside, the capital structure is doing what capital structures do: rewriting the company's future choices.

Debt doesn't just change the balance sheet; it changes the house rules:

- **Covenant creep.** Maintenance covenants, incurrence tests, "restricted payments" baskets, and springing leverage ratios quietly rewire decision rights. You can do almost anything, until a metric crosses a line no customer has ever cared about.

Then "capital returns" become a memory and "restricted payments" a vocabulary lesson.

- **Refinancing dependence.** Short maturities look prudent until the cycle turns. Rolling paper is easy when everyone believes tomorrow will be like today. When spreads widen, strategy becomes the calendar of your maturities. The product roadmap now fits inside a debt ladder.
- **Ratings as policy.** Credit ratings migrate from commentary to commandment. "Protect the grade" becomes a strategic imperative that outranks platform bets. Agencies don't run your business, but their math starts to.
- **SBC alchemy.** Equity comp is pitched as alignment and quietly neutralized with debt-funded buybacks "to offset dilution." Cash that could have built capacity buys the illusion that no dilution occurred. The P&L looks unruffled; the balance sheet absorbed the truth.

Leverage also distorts the supply chain. Working capital becomes a piggy bank: payables stretch, inventory buffers thin, vendor financing fills gaps that used to be covered by competence. Fragility compounds in places the EPS slide does not measure, single-source dependencies, longer lead times, higher breakage when something upstream sneezes. The numbers hold steady until they don't.

The EPS lift is immediate; the cost arrives later and irregularly:

- **Rate regime whiplash.** Floating tranches reprice faster than pricing power. The first thing sacrificed is the spend with no defender in the next quarter, tooling, reliability work, platform refactors, the exact investments that would have made pricing power real.

- **Liquidity mirage.** Cash looks ample because the revolver is undrawn. Then a hiccup, a recall, a cyber event, a regulatory hold, eats the cushion. Suddenly "optionality" means negotiating waivers at 2 a.m. with lenders who have veto power over your strategy.
- **Pension and lease shadows.** Long-dated obligations that never made the EPS slide, pensions, operating leases, take-or-pay contracts, behave like invisible leverage. When volatility hits, they move from shadow to spotlight and crowd out oxygen you thought you had.

The culture shifts with the structure. Leaders who once argued about customers now argue about baskets and headroom. Product reviews include a slide called "capital implications," translated as: will this trigger a covenant? The smartest financial operators rise; the loudest builders leave. Nobody decided to privilege creditors over customers; the indenture did.

Debt also changes the meaning of time. Invention needs slack; leverage monetizes slack. The organization becomes exquisitely punctual in the wrong dimension. Cash interest is due on the day it's due. Principal is due on the day it's due. Learning is due when it's ready, but learning now answers to a calendar that doesn't believe in it. When the crunch comes, the knife never finds PR or IR first. It finds the programs that can't defend themselves in a quarter.

There is a particular quiet moment when the disguise fails. It doesn't look like panic; it looks like "prudence." Hiring freezes arrive. "Nonessential" travel and testing pause. "Phase two" becomes "phase never." Capital committees meet more often and approve less. Everyone repeats the same sentence, *we're being disciplined*, as if discipline were a synonym for retreat. EPS still looks intact. Capability does not.

On the way up, leverage flatters management. On the way down, it governs them. Maturities dictate what gets sold. Covenants dictate who gets paid. Ratings dictate where you can compete. The company that once told a story about its products now tells a story about its capital structure and calls it strategy.

There are softer disguises, too:

- **Securitizations and factoring.** Receivables are turned into today's cash and tomorrow's hole. Days sales outstanding improve; customer quality does not.
- **Vendor "partnerships."** Extended terms feel like strength until the vendor reprices risk or finds a better customer. The supply chain's patience is leverage you don't control.
- **Capitalized everything.** Costs migrate to assets where depreciation will politely smooth them. The smoothing is elegant. The physics it conceals are not.

Leverage is not a sin. The disguise is. When debt funds optics, it converts volatility into a promise the business hasn't earned. The balance sheet looks athletic in formalwear; the operating system underneath wheezes. The bill doesn't arrive as a single catastrophe. It arrives as a decade you can't afford to build, because you spent the last one renting your stock.

SBC Alchemy

It begins in a conference room with soft chairs and harder numbers. The comp committee nods through another deck about "alignment." Equity, they're told, is how a company turns employees into owners. The logic is clean: pay in stock, conserve cash, tie upside to outcomes. Heads nod. The story feels right because it is, until the second story arrives.

The second story lives a few floors down, in finance. There, someone points at the share count. Dilution, they say gently, will trouble the street. The solution is equally gentle: we'll buy back the shares we just issued. No one calls it a loop; everyone calls it discipline. In the earnings script, the sentences sit two paragraphs apart. "We continue to invest in our people." Later: "We offset dilution through repurchases." The words never touch. The cash does.

On paper, it is elegant. SBC runs through GAAP like a fine print confession; adjusted earnings invite it back out the door. The repurchase keeps per-share neatness intact. Labor looks cheap in the income statement, expensive in the cash flow, and invisible in the EPS slide. The chart smiles. The company congratulates itself on alignment.

Inside the building, alignment means something else. It means the stock becomes weather. Teams learn the seasons: blackout, open window, investor day. Announcements are timed accordingly. Bad news drifts to the corners of the calendar where it will cast the smallest shadow on vest dates. Good news blooms where it can be harvested. The calendar of liquidity begins to outrank the calendar of customers.

Engineers sense it first. They used to work to the rhythm of prototypes and field data. Now there is a second drum: windows, cliffs, refresh cycles. Conversations shift from "What did we learn?" to "When can we talk about it?" The answers are rarely technical. A promising fix slips, not because it is wrong, but because the quarter is wrong. No one says this aloud. The team says "we'll sequence it." The word is sterile enough to pass in any meeting.

Grant statements arrive like postcards from a future that may or may not happen. Some employees pin them above their desks; others learn not to look directly at hypotheticals. When the stock runs, belief surges. When it sinks, the company reprices, the language softens, and trust becomes an accrual no one can amortize. People tell themselves they're here for the mission, and many are, but missions share space with mortgages. The slide that says "ownership mentality" does not mention daycare.

Managers acquire a new skill: grant diplomacy. They parcel refresh like rations, smoothing discontent, deferring departures, quieting the talented with promises inked in vest schedules. The most valuable people begin to look like the ones who can navigate the pool, not the ones who can bend the physics. Performance reviews absorb comp strategy like tea absorbs sugar. Sweetness hides the taste of the water.

On the street, the company speaks a different dialect. "Profit excluding SBC," it says, as if compensation were an idea and not a transfer. Analysts nod. Models hum. The buyback line swells with confidence: "offsetting dilution." The sentence lands clean because it erases two truths at once, that equity was a cost, and that the cash now missing could have built something besides a chart.

Down in operations, the distortion shows up as silence. A launch that needs another month gets shipped because the window is open. A risky subsystem that would slash unit costs at scale is rephrased into phases that never quite reach the phase where courage is required. "Accretive this year" becomes the invisible brief for work that should be measured in durability, not deniability. Everyone understands, because everyone can read a vest schedule.

Blackout rules harden into habit. People learn to carry ideas across quiet periods like contraband, declaring nothing until disclosure is legal. Strategy begins to follow HR calendars: cliffs spike attrition; teams go thin; the survivors hold their breath until refresh day. This is not policy. It is physics. Incentives have mass.

There is a quarter when the trick feels perfect. SBC is high because the company is growing; adjusted profit shines because the company is disciplined; the buyback is large because the balance sheet is "efficient." In the transcript, these things do not touch. In the real company, they touch everywhere. Cash that might have thickened reliability is now a promise that the share count won't grow. Equity that was supposed to be ownership is now a number the company spends to pretend ownership was free.

The longer it runs, the stranger it gets. Overhang swells, years of grants accumulating into a future tax on hiring no one budgets for. Burn rate looks "in range," but no one can quite say what the burn bought. The town hall speaks of "investing in people," but the graph that matters is the slope of adoption or the fall of defect rates, instruments that do not appear on compensation slides. Somewhere, a senior engineer notices they have become a custodian of sentiment. They did not come to the company to study sentiment.

And then there is the day the stock breaks under the weight of something unrelated, a macro wobble, a missed forecast, a competitor's surprise. Options go underwater. Refresh becomes triage. Repricing arrives like a weather alert: we're stabilizing morale. People are grateful and resentful at the same time. The gesture fixes math, not belief. You cannot reprice the feeling that your work is indexed to a line you do not control.

The organization's voice adapts. It speaks more softly near windows. It chooses safer verbs. It learns to hide the rough edges of reality inside phrases that feel like progress: "balanced framework," "responsible cadence," "offsetting dilution." The words do their job. They smooth. They reassure. They erase.

What they cannot erase is the slow tilt of attention from customers to cadence, from physics to performance, from building to narrating. The company still talks about innovation. It hosts a demo day. It puts "owner" on the wall in a font large enough to read from the back row. People clap. They go back to their desks. They check a number that moves more than their code.

SBC was supposed to align everyone to value. In practice, it aligns everyone to visibility. It turns the stock into weather and weather into policy. It teaches smart people to time truth. It builds a culture fluent in the management of appearance and careful around the edges where capability is earned.

No one set out to do this. It happened one neat quarter at a time, with language that felt responsible and math that felt clean. The illusion held because it was tidy. The cost hid because it was everywhere else.

Example: Snowflake, SBC as Operating System

It starts with a promise that feels harmless: pay in equity because talent is the product. RSUs become the default language of offers and refresh, a currency everyone in the building understands. On the slides, SBC is "non-cash," a footnote you reconcile away in non-GAAP. In the labs, it's how you hire, retain, and pace the roadmap.

By fiscal 2025, the scale is no longer abstract, Snowflake's stock-based compensation ran above $1.5 billion, roughly 43% of revenue that year. That's not a rounding error; that's a center of gravity.

You can watch the ramp in the filings. Coming out of hypergrowth, SBC moved from $862 million (FY2023) to $1.17 billion (FY2024), then higher again into FY2025, even as product revenue matured. The company's own releases frame the top line, FY2023 product revenue $1.9B; FY2025 quarterly product revenue pacing in the high-$900Ms per quarter, but the culture feels the line item more than the headline: equity is how the place breathes.

Inside, SBC sets the calendar. Grant cliffs shape when people ship and when they leave; blackout windows quietly dictate when truth can be told. When the stock runs, morale is oxygen; when it stalls, refresh diplomacy takes over: managers huddle to keep keystone builders whole without blowing burn. The effect is behavioral, not just financial, teams begin timing reveals to vesting rhythm, and product reviews inherit a new question: not only "is it ready?" but "when does it land relative to grants?" (No slide will ever say this; the hallway will.)

SBC also rewires what "profitable" means. GAAP shows the expense; non-GAAP adds it back; the narrative emphasizes efficiency while the engineering backlog still wants cash and time. The result is a split-screen reality: a company that *must* keep issuing equity to compete for talent at scale, and a workforce whose compensation, and patience, rises and falls with a ticker. As the SBC share of revenue sits in the ~40% zip code, every platform refactor, reliability push, or unit-cost bend competes not only with dollars but with dilution math embedded in planning.

None of this is an indictment of the tool; it's a description of the system it creates. When SBC is the oxygen, hiring is fast, refresh is policy, and time itself gets priced in grants. The filings give you the numbers, \$862M → \$1.17B → >\$1.5B; the press releases give you the revenue; the culture supplies the rest: a cadence where compensation mechanics start to steer product tempo as much as customers do. That's SBC as operating system, powerful, necessary, and, at scale, determinative.

Manufacturing the Launch

A date gets chosen before the product is durable, and the company quietly rearranges itself around the calendar. Messaging locks before capability; names, logos, and motion graphics harden while systems are still negotiating with physics. Demos are engineered to follow a golden path, QA narrows to "don't embarrass us on stage," and decisions are framed by embargoes, blackout windows, and earnings week proximity. The show lands: the video hits, the live graph climbs, the hashtag trends, and the transcript earns its tidy paragraph about "overwhelming interest."

Then reality arrives without choreography. Real users click out of sequence, bring unruly data, and traverse edge cases that were deferred to "post-launch hardening." Adoption spikes flatten into the slope you must earn; cohort tables whisper churn while dashboards celebrate impressions. Support queues reveal patterns no keynote can: latency under load, brittle integrations, reliability that only exists on stage. The true second launch, when reliability holds, macros retire, and sales no longer needs an engineer in the room, comes quietly at 2 a.m., unphotogenic but decisive.

Manufacturing the launch also manufactures debt. Technical debt from patches that bought applause; operational debt from processes trained to serve events; cultural debt from teaching the company that a good day is trending, not durable. Telltales accumulate: instrumentation added late, feature flags that never come down, GA with caveats, postmortems that critique stagecraft more than systems. Repeat the cycle and the organization becomes excellent at days and average at years, fluent at shipping keynotes, thin at shipping moats, until the market stops mistaking performance for progress.

Vendor and Supply-Chain Myopia

It starts tidy: stretch payables, trim inventory, "do more with the base." Cash conversion improves, suppliers smile politely, nothing breaks, so the habit hardens. Dual-sourcing is deferred, buffers thin, freight shifts to spot. From a distance the chain looks elegant; up close it's a high wire with no net.

Suppliers read capital signals. The best quietly rebalance away from customers who treat them like banks. Lead times lengthen, A-teams rotate off your account, quality drifts at the edges, parts pass spec, fail in the field. Purchasing still books "savings"; goodwill, unmeasured, runs down. Concentration risk hides until a regional hiccup, weather, strike, politics, turns one favored vendor into a single point of failure. Expedites become routine; planners live in war rooms; margin holds for a quarter while fatigue and errors accumulate off-slide.

Financial plumbing masks the strain. Reverse factoring keeps your DPO immaculate while small vendors subsidize your neatness with their liquidity. Some hold back capacity; some exit. Under pressure, shadows appear: gray-market parts, "equivalents" that fit until they don't. ESG slides stay clean; support lines do not.

Telltales are consistent: vendor reviews become term fights, NCRs rise as closure slows, "forecast accuracy" improves by narrowing to what finance prefers, and the list of partners who answer after hours gets short. Each decision was rational in isolation, one more week of terms, one more cut to safety stock, until a shock arrives and the mirror cracks, revealing what the numbers hid: a chain optimized for quarters, brittle for reality.

M&A Substitution

It begins as a shortcut with a spreadsheet halo. The roadmap is lumpy, the quarter is near, and a banker arrives with something smoother than invention: *accretion*. A "tuck-in" that adds revenue on day one, a bolt-on that promises "synergies," a slide where EPS rises obediently in the rightmost column. Inside the room, people who distrust uncertainty finally have a way to buy motion without making any.

The hygiene looks impeccable. Pro formas hum. "Non-GAAP accretive in year one," the deck says, as if advantage were a meter you can plug into a wall. Diligence piles up exactly where it's easiest: historicals, cohorts, churn masks, pipeline aging, a list of customers who say they'll stay if nothing changes, which is the one thing that always changes. Someone presents "technology fit" on a single slide. The word *fit* does a lot of work.

Deal heat replaces product heat. Calendars shift from releases to regulatory filings, from milestones to milestones, the kind you announce to investors, not to customers. Integration plans are born as checklists: Day 0 comms, Day 30 brand, Day 60 systems cutover.

The PMO prints dashboards that glow green because the tasks are tidy: emails sent, domains redirected, HRIS merged. None of those tasks bend a cost curve or deepen a moat, but all of them finish on time.

Meanwhile, the product multiplies faster than the platform. SKUs proliferate; brochures outpace code. Sales is taught to "solution sell" across a catalog that now needs a field guide. Bundles appear to hide seams. Cross-sell quotas make numbers go up and NPS go down. Support learns three ticketing systems. Engineers learn three architectures. The company learns the difference between owning and integrating.

The cultural debt is slower and more expensive than the purchase price. The acquired team arrived to build; they are put to work being acquired. Their roadmap, once a promise to customers, becomes a negotiation with committees. The best people leave first and quietly, taking the reason you bought the company with them. HR calls it regrettable attrition; finance calls it synergies realized. Accounting calls it goodwill.

Goodwill is a kind word for the amount you couldn't explain. It sits on the balance sheet like a compliment you hope to deserve later. When the market turns or the thesis ages, impairment converts the unsaid into the undeniable. The write-down will be labeled "non-cash," which is true in the quarter and false across the years you lost building the things you tried to buy.

Serial acquirers develop a reflex: when the roadmap stalls, look outside. The banker pipeline becomes more legible than the product pipeline. Off-sites discuss "addressable market" more than addressable physics. The organization forgets muscles it once had, decision speed, integration craft, the patience to make one thing great, because those muscles atrophy when the fastest wins are on closing dates.

Customers notice in the seams. Contracts get re-papered; support scripts lengthen; features promised as "better together" remain merely adjacent. The integration demo is carefully narrated; the live environment is not. Renewal conversations become about bundles and discounts instead of outcomes. You have more to sell and less to stand on.

Rates rise and the habit shows its cost. What was "low-cost capital" becomes a debt ladder dictating priorities. Deals that were justified on cost of funds now live under covenants and rating agency memos. The calendar of maturities, not the calendar of learning, tells the company what it can afford to be.

None of this looks reckless while it's happening. Each acquisition makes sense in isolation: logical adjacency, talented team, "plug and play." The pattern becomes visible only when the catalog grows fat and the platform stays thin, when green dashboards from the integration office coexist with red tables from customer success, when the share price reflects a portfolio and the market asks to see a product.

M&A was supposed to accelerate the strategy. Done as substitution, it *becomes* the strategy. The company gets excellent at buying stories and average at finishing them. The pitch never changes: *this one is different*. The outcome rarely does.

The Activist Investor

An activist investor is a shareholder, often a hedge fund or special-situations firm, that buys a meaningful stake (typically 1–10%) not to own the company, but to influence how it is run. Influence is the product. They campaign, publicly or privately, for actions that move the stock in a near-to-medium window: cost cuts, asset sales or spins, reshaping the board, executive changes, divestitures, dividend hikes, and especially larger, faster "returns of capital" (buybacks). They don't need control; they need leverage, votes, media, proxy advisers, and a plan the market will price immediately.

They differ from traditional long-only owners in time horizon and tactics. Where an institutional holder negotiates quietly and waits, the activist compresses time: open letters, slide decks, media rounds, proxy contests, and settlement threats. Where private equity seeks control and long operational work, the activist seeks outcomes without ownership, re-pricing the equity by forcing visible moves the market rewards.

Common species:

- **Operational activists:** push margin targets, SG&A cuts, footprint "rationalization," R&D "focus."
- **Financial engineers:** demand spins, sum-of-the-parts breakups, lever-up-and-return-cash programs.
- **Governance reformers:** board refreshes, executive comp redesign, anti-poison-pill, de-staggered boards.
- **Event catalysts:** agitate for a sale or "strategic alternatives" when standalone value won't re-rate fast enough.

Primary tools:

- **Stake + letter:** a public thesis that frames underperformance and a "clear path" to unlock value.
- **Proxy pressure:** nominating directors, courting proxy advisors (ISS/Glass Lewis), rallying passive funds.

- **Media narrative:** turning a plan into a stock story, tidy charts, peer comps, TSR league tables.
- **Settlement leverage:** extracting board seats and commitments without a full-blown vote.

Tell-tale signals inside a company:

- Board decks open with TSR and "peer medians" before product reality.
- Phrases like *strategic alternatives, non-core, right-size, return of excess capital* migrate into every meeting.
- Roadmaps become triage lists that fit inside quarters; ambiguity is treated as malpractice.

That's the definition and the posture: a shareholder whose business model is time, shortening it, pricing it, weaponizing it, so that what could have been a multi-year strategy is forced into a sequence the market will applaud now.

The Activist as Innovation's Antithesis

They don't arrive as villains. They arrive as adults in the room, polite decks, clean verbs, tidy charts that promise discipline. And yet, almost perfectly, their remedies cancel the conditions innovation needs. Not by decree, by design. Innovation feeds on slack, ambiguity, and lumpy timelines; activism weaponizes schedules, certainties, and smooth lines. Put them in the same building and one will starve the other without anyone raising their voice.

The activist compresses time. What was a multi-year capability becomes a quarterly performance. Stage gates harden to prevent variance on the call, not to protect learning in the lab. Budgets aren't "cut," they're "re-prioritized" toward the accretive and away from the compounding. Platform work gets sliced into phases that never reach the phase where it stops being cost and starts being advantage. Exploration is relabeled "non-core", a category where bets go to be quietly postponed into irrelevance.

People adapt, which is the problem. Builders learn to present like bankers. The most rewarded skill becomes removing surprise from transcripts rather than from systems. Attrition rises where audacity lived; it looks small in a metric and enormous in a crisis. Suppliers feel the chill, buffers thin, dual sources wait, resilience is renamed "waste." The chain works until it doesn't, and the memo calls it macro.

Language completes the inversion. "Focus" comes to mean "do fewer safe things." "Unlock value" means "sell optionality." "Efficiency" means "no slack for discovery." None of this is malicious; it's mechanical. The activist optimizes the surface, cash, margins, governance, precisely where innovation cannot live. The stock pops. The labs go quiet. Everyone did the reasonable thing, and the unreasonable thing, the breakthrough, lost by forfeit.

That is why activism, even well-intended, is innovation's opposite. Innovation asks for patience, variance, and nerve; activism prices impatience, punishes variance, and rewards caution. One builds moats you can't narrate yet. The other narrates outcomes you haven't built. Put them on the same clock, and the clock wins.

Procter & Gamble: When Activism Meets the Lab

The letter landed first, then the headlines, then the recount: Nelson Peltz wins a P&G board seat by just 43,000 votes (0.002%), a photo-finish that still rewrites posture inside the building. Business Insider In the board deck, red boxes give way to a tidy plan: simplify the portfolio, raise margins, return more cash. Much of it was already in motion, P&G had started a purge years earlier, but the arrival of an activist turns tempo into mandate.

The simplification was real and large. Management set out to shed 90–100 brands, keeping 70–80 that drove ~90% of sales and 95%+ of profit; centerpiece: a $12.5B Reverse Morris Trust to spin 43 beauty brands (Max Factor, CoverGirl, licensed fragrances) into Coty. License Global+4Bloomberg+4Fortune+4 At the same time, the cost machine tightened. A first $10B productivity program (2012–2016) rolled through COGS, overhead, and media; by 2016 P&G was signaling another $10B, ultimately citing $23B in cumulative savings and 12,600 non-manufacturing roles eliminated. Structure followed story: in 2019, the company shifted to six sector business units, leaner spans, faster calls. Marketing Dive

On the transcript, it worked. Organic sales growth ran 5%, 6%, 6%, 7%, 7% from FY2019–FY2023; e-commerce crossed $10B (≈14% of sales) with +35% growth in FY2021; free-cash-flow productivity printed 95–114%; the dividend lifted +10% in 2021, the largest increase in a decade. Margins cleaned up too, operating margin near the ~22% band in recent years after a messy 2019 write-down year, exactly the kind of neatness activists promise. Companies Market Cap

Inside the labs, the trade-offs showed up in subtler math. In FY2020, R&D fell 60 bps to 4.3% of sales, a small line that carries a long echo in categories where compounding comes from formulation, packaging science, and manufacturing tricks you can't narrate in a quarter. The new six-unit cadence made "focus" a daily discipline; it also made "phase it" the default for lumpy platform bets. When a fabric-care team argued to fund an ugly year of base-chemistry retooling, the kind that bends unit costs for a decade, the room asked a rational question learned from the deck: could it be sequenced to hit accretion targets first? Sequenced meant sliced; sliced meant delayed. The SKU tree grew tidier while the moat grew mostly by price/mix. (In FY2023, organic +8% could be broken into +7% pricing and +2% mix against –1% volume, an arithmetic that flatters the call more than the formulation bench.) Investopedia

None of this paints villains. The portfolio got simpler, cash got crisper, and growth revived, facts you can't hand-wave. But it also shows how activism's clock can become the company's clock. The brand cuts and $10B+ savings were legible immediately; the chemistry and process work that makes Tide or Pampers uncopyable asks for patience measured in cycles, not quarters. When the vote is decided by 0.002%, you learn to keep time to the market's metronome. The numbers printed beautifully. The question innovation people still ask is the one that never prints: What did we postpone to make them print this well, this fast?

Twitter : Activism's Clock (Narrative, with numbers)

The campaign arrived as a collaboration: in March 2020 Twitter struck a truce with Elliott Management and Silver Lake, $1B from Silver Lake, $2B in authorized buybacks, two new directors (Egon Durban, Jesse Cohn), and a leadership/governance review committee. It looked tidy on paper: capital, board refresh, "discipline." The point wasn't ownership; it was time, compressing outcomes into a window the market would immediately price

Twelve months later, the clock had a voice. Ahead of its 2021 investor day, Twitter pledged to at least double revenue from $3.7B (2020) to $7.5B+ by 2023 and reach 315M mDAU by Q4 2023, targets that traveled beautifully on a call and landed like deadlines inside product and trust & safety teams. In 2021, revenue did jump to ~$5.1B (+37% YoY), and mDAU kept climbing (e.g., 187M in Q3'20; 192M in Q4'20), but the promise now ran faster than the plumbing. The roadmap felt less like invention and more like cadence.

Governance followed the tempo. In November 2021, Jack Dorsey stepped down; CTO Parag Agrawal became CEO, another neat outcome the market could price. By February 2022, the board authorized a $4B repurchase, including a $2B accelerated share repurchase, EPS-friendly signals that reinforced the new metronome. The activist didn't dictate features; the balance between narrative and capability shifted anyway

From the outside, the story read as momentum. From the inside, compression showed up in choices: performance ads and SMB monetization moved to the front of the line (legible, near-term), while slower compounding work, reliability at scale, developer platform depth, safety systems that reduce moderation drag, competed with the calendar. The numbers kept printing, but the slope was fragile: after 2021's $5.1B peak, post-deal turmoil would see revenue falter industry-wide; the pre-sale targets (315M mDAU, $7.5B 2023) were never tested as a standalone path. Activism hadn't "killed innovation"; it re-priced it, turning multi-year capability into quarterly performance and leaving the platform fluent in promises the system hadn't fully earned.

The CEO's Dilemma: Vision on a Clock

It looks like power from the outside. From the inside, it feels like triage. A CEO is hired to move a company across decades and measured on what happens in ninety days. Every lever that builds the future, platform rewrites, supply resilience, brand reinvention, talent compounding, demands time and ambiguity. Every lever that calms the present, buybacks, "focus," cost programs, manufactured launches, pays immediately. The board says "both." The calendar says "choose."

Compensation doesn't help. Packages tilt toward stock outcomes that can be managed faster than moats can be built. The vesting clock hums under every decision review; the share-count slide arrives before the customer slide. Investor days reward sentences, not systems; "proof points" become choreography. The question inside the room is rarely "Is this the right architecture?" It's "Can we narrate it by Q4?"

The board wants courage with no variance. They ask for a bold plan that won't miss guidance, a replatform that won't dent gross margin, a portfolio surgery that won't bruise cash flow. Governance frameworks multiply to prevent "surprises," which is where invention lives. A CEO learns the grammar of safety: *sequence, phase, re-prioritize*. The verbs are true and lethal. They turn a vision into installments that never reach the installment where advantage compounds.

Activists don't have to win seats to change posture. A single public letter shortens horizons without touching the org chart. Proxy advisors nod, passive funds nod, headlines nod. The CEO feels it in IR prep: TSR first, peers second, customers third. A sensible hedge emerges, move the numbers you can move while protecting the bets you can't explain yet. The hedge calcifies into a plan. The plan becomes identity.

Inside the company, truth starts to keep the market's hours. Bad news waits for blackout; good news blooms near windows. Launches orbit earnings week. "Post-launch hardening" drifts to the quarter after the call. Even the sincere long-term bets are re-cut to fit the transcript. The CEO isn't lying; they're translating, turning a multi-year slope into quarters that look like progress. The translation taxes the thing being translated.

The human cost lands last. Builders who thrive on difficult slopes notice that the CEO's job has become performance management for the stock. They don't blame the person; they blame the clock. Some stay and adapt, sanding edges off proposals until they pass. Others leave for places where time is oxygen. A CEO can feel the talent shift before the metrics do: meetings get quieter at the edges where audacity used to live.

And then there is the night every CEO remembers: the choice between the ugly year that fixes the engine and the beautiful year that fixes the slide. One creates variance now and compounding later. The other delivers applause now and obligation later. Both are defensible. Only one survives a transcript. The dilemma is not a failure of will; it's a system that prices nerve as risk and neatness as leadership.

There are CEOs who thread it, who protect a few sacred, lumpy bets while feeding the quarterly machine just enough to keep it docile. But threading is not the same as freedom. It is leadership on a narrow bridge: one eye on physics, one eye on optics, and wind from both sides. We'll save prescriptions for later. For now, it's enough to name the bind: vision measured in decades, judged in weeks, translated into quarters, and too often postponed into never.

Example : Steve Jobs (Apple, 1985): Vision on a Short Clock

Spring–summer 1985: Apple posts its first quarterly loss, $17.2 million, and announces 1,200 layoffs plus the closure of 3 of 6 plants. Markets, media, and directors want stability; predictability suddenly outranks audacity. In the power struggle that follows, the board sides with CEO John Sculley and strips Jobs of operational control; by September, Jobs resigns. The proximate cause was governance conflict, but the backdrop was unmistakable: a company under short-term pressure choosing near-term steadiness over the leader arguing for uncomfortable reinvention.

Context matters. Macintosh sales were below early hopes, and the board, staring at fresh losses and factory closures, opted for the safer narrative and a tighter operating grip. Jobs' removal wasn't a referendum on invention; it was a decision to de-risk the next few quarters, even if it meant ejecting the long-horizon architect. History is the footnote: Jobs left to found NeXT, Apple later re-acquired that technology, bringing Jobs back in 1997, and the platform he'd been building outside became the foundation of Apple's modern OS and product run. Short-term calm won the meeting; long-term compounding won the decade

Conclusion: When the Quarter Becomes the Company

It doesn't announce itself with a crisis. It arrives as competence: EPS exactly on script, a buyback that irons noise into neatness, leverage that flatters ratios, launches that land on cue, "focus" that turns mess into bullet points. One by one, reasonable choices stack into an unreasonable system. Denominator management stands in for growth. SBC becomes the air supply. Debt makes fragility look formal. Supply chains are tuned like violins until the string snaps. M&A supplies catalog mass in place of platform slope. Activists

132

compress time until learning has nowhere left to live. Nothing explodes; compounding just quietly stops.

This is the shareholder trap operating at peak efficiency: arithmetic substituting for advantage. The numbers are immaculate, the narrative frictionless, the cadence comforting. The invoice comes in a currency the transcript doesn't track, optionalities not taken, buffers not bought, refactors not funded, hires who never joined, builders who left without a scene. By the time the market asks for something only a long horizon can produce, the organization speaks finance more fluently than physics, cadence more fluently than craft.

What follows is a company optimized to *report* value rather than create it. Roadmaps narrow to what can be narrated; courage is rescheduled; reliability is promised later; customers feel the stillness first. Inside, reviews evolve from "Are we getting better?" to "Are we on plan?" Outside, competitors ship the unphotogenic work that bends curves over years. The scoreboard stays green, until green stops mattering.

Look closely at the wreckage and you won't find villains, only incentives that did their job too well. Buybacks that proved discipline also priced out discovery. SBC that aligned talent also turned truth into a calendar. Debt that seemed cheap sold future slack at a discount. "Focus" that cleaned the portfolio also amputated the awkward limbs where breakthroughs usually grow. Manufactured launches gave the appearance of momentum while the engine idled.

And yet, the story doesn't end at the waterline of Wall Street. Even if the market were patient, many companies would still run aground on their own internal geography. That's where we go next: The Silo Effect, the quiet architecture that breaks judgment into pieces. Silos don't just separate teams; they separate truth from context. Product from customer. Factory from finance. Data from decision. They turn translation into a tax and handoffs into blind spots. If the quarter narrows *time*, silos narrow *understanding*. Together they produce the same outcome: an organization superb at avoiding surprise and poor at creating the future.

In the next chapter, we'll walk the corridors between those walls, where metrics are laundered into approval, where incentives mutate information, where interfaces become battlegrounds, and where the best ideas die not in opposition but in transit. The market's impatience is one trap. The company's own map is another.

CHAPTER 5

The Silo Effect: How Internal Walls Slow the Future

The Anatomy of Disconnect

A product always begins with clarity, a handful of people in a room, a whiteboard, a clean problem. For a moment, everyone can see the same future. Then the room empties, and the idea starts to cool.

Engineering takes it to ensure feasibility. Marketing takes it to shape the story. Program management takes it to protect the calendar. Each act is responsible. Each one adds structure. And with each layer, the idea loses a few degrees of heat.

By the time the sketch becomes a roadmap, the language has splintered. Engineering speaks in tickets and dependencies. Marketing speaks in headlines and hooks. Design speaks in flows. Project management speaks in dates. They all use the same nouns, *launch, performance, experience*, but the meanings no longer align.

In the first sprint, everyone still feels the spark: *make it faster, simpler, better*. But friction hides in translation. Marketing wants the feature that demos beautifully. Design wants the flow that feels human. Firmware wants the architecture that never fails. Product wants it all inside the quarter. None are wrong. Together, they are impossible.

Even within engineering, the seams multiply. Electrical, mechanical, and software teams build to spec, each spec accurate alone and incompatible together. Interfaces meet on paper, clash in prototype, and settle into compromise by production. The result works perfectly in parts and awkwardly as a whole: a machine that passes validation but fails to sing.

Integration becomes ceremony. Teams sync by ticket instead of instinct. Review meetings replace collaboration. What once felt like invention starts to feel like obligation, progress tracked in slides rather than curiosity shared in rooms.

By launch, every chart glows green. The metrics are tidy. The dashboards hum. But inside the team, celebration feels forced. The product is good, and that's the problem. It's good in a way that feels smaller than it should, precise but lifeless. It was built exactly as planned and nothing more.

Innovation rarely collapses in catastrophe; it fades in calibration. It dies not because anyone stopped caring, but because everyone cared about different things, in different directions, at slightly different speeds.

No villains. No rebellion. Just distance, the quiet space between people who used to finish each other's sentences and now send each other updates. The space where potential turns procedural, where invention learns to wait its turn.

The tragedy is that none of this looks broken. From inside, the machinery hums. Teams deliver. Reviews close. Dashboards climb. But the pulse that once united the work, a shared sense of purpose, a rhythm that crossed disciplines, no longer moves through the system. What began as a single project's coordination problem becomes the company's way of breathing: polite handoffs instead of collisions, meetings instead of momentum. Innovation doesn't vanish; it's dispersed, stretched thin across calendars, approvals, and careful updates until motion itself becomes fragmented. And once fragmentation becomes normal, it stops belonging to projects. It becomes culture.

That's where the damage compounds: when silos stop being symptoms and start being architecture.

Silos in Motion

Silos rarely announce themselves. They don't crash into a company as villains; they grow quietly, camouflaged as structure. At first, they look like maturity, clearer roles, tidy budgets, clean lines of accountability. But what begins as order becomes insulation. Departments that were meant to specialize begin to territorialize. The walls built to protect efficiency start to absorb energy instead of conducting it. What was once an organism becomes a collection of parts politely coexisting.

Innovation doesn't die in these moments, it suffocates. It happens one well-meaning policy at a time, one careful gate review, one "alignment" meeting that spends more time harmonizing metrics than moving them. No one declares the company risk-averse; it just learns to walk slower, to defer friction, to value precision over possibility. The silence is the signal.

Take any large development project. At the start, there's alignment, a clear goal, a whiteboard, an almost electric sense of potential. Engineering sketches a path, product defines outcomes, marketing begins to shape the narrative. But as the idea travels, the distance begins to show. Engineering optimizes for feasibility, marketing for story, project management for schedule, finance for predictability. None of these are wrong, but together they stretch the idea until it loses heat. What began as a living system, a product, slowly decomposes into a set of subsystems, each flawless in isolation, disconnected in purpose.

It's rarely incompetence. It's geometry. The more nodes in the network, the more translation between them, the more meaning is lost in transit. The learning loop that was supposed to tighten becomes a pipeline with latency. The product that should breathe like a single machine starts to behave like components wired by committee. And by the time it ships, the only thing connecting the parts is the PowerPoint that justified them.

Inside large corporations, this pattern feels normal, even professional. Engineers say "that's not my scope." Marketing says "we weren't looped in early enough." Operations says "we hit our SLA." Everyone's right, but the result is wrong. Each team defends its green metrics, while the system turns gray. Progress still happens, but without coherence; motion without music.

The truth is that silos don't kill projects dramatically, they bleed them slowly. The loss doesn't show up on a dashboard; it lives in the pauses between messages, the rework after a late discovery, the quiet frustration of smart people watching their work collide midair. In highly matrixed organizations, even within engineering, one group optimizes for performance, another for maintainability, another for compliance. Each discipline builds its own masterpiece, but together they form an orchestra that never tunes to the same key.

The result is a kind of invisible friction, the tax of translation. Every new interface between teams is another place the idea must survive interpretation. Words like "launch," "activation," and "user" begin to mean different things in different rooms. Meetings end with alignment that exists only linguistically. People nod to the same nouns while thinking different verbs.

Eventually, the product reflects the conversation that built it, precise, well-structured, and oddly lifeless. The customer experiences a machine designed by distance: an app that's beautiful but inconsistent, a service that's fast but impersonal, a system that works but never delights. It's not broken; it's bureaucratically perfect.

No one meant for this to happen. Every decision was rational. Every team delivered its piece on time. But the seams between those pieces told another story, one of latency, duplication, and lost intent. Somewhere between the kickoff and the launch, the company's curiosity was converted into compliance. The energy that once flowed freely now recirculates through status updates and steering decks.

That's how silos kill, not with failure, but with plausible success. The initiative ships. The metrics trend in acceptable directions. The post-mortem finds nothing technically wrong. Yet something fundamental is missing: the spark of coherence, the sense that everyone was building the same thing for the same reason. The company didn't reject innovation; it simply exhausted it in transit.

This quiet erosion repeats across every function, a sales team protecting its funnel, a data team safeguarding its definitions, a product team managing its roadmap. Each local optimization accumulates global degradation. The seams widen, ownership diffuses, and every improvement gets smaller than the problem it was meant to solve. The company becomes a federation of competence that somehow fails to produce greatness.

And because nothing visibly breaks, no one sounds the alarm. The business still grows. The charts still rise. The decks still glow with color. But the slope flattens, imperceptibly at first. By the time anyone notices, the gap between what's possible and what's permitted has become the real measure of distance.

Silos do not end innovation in a crash; they end it in equilibrium. Everything continues to move, but nothing moves the whole. That is how the future slows, quietly, through systems that are too careful to fail and too divided to fly.

The Hidden Ledger

Every company keeps two sets of books. The official one balances perfectly, budgets align, headcount is justified, milestones glow green. It's the version shown to boards, analysts, and all-hands meetings: a portrait of order and progress. But beneath it lies another ledger, the one no system tracks, where the real costs of motion live. It records time lost to translation, intent lost to approval, choices deferred until they disappear. Its currency isn't dollars or euros but days, clarity, and trust. And though no one audits it, this is the ledger that quietly determines whether a company is accelerating or aging in place.

Time is the first entry. Every handoff, review, and alignment call adds invisible days to the calendar. Work that should take twelve weeks becomes sixteen, then twenty, not through negligence but through coordination. Everyone delivers on time inside their lane; collectively, the organization moves late. Urgency gets traded for choreography. Velocity doesn't vanish in the work itself; it evaporates in the corridors between it.

Then comes the loss of meaning. Every idea begins sharp, alive, and slightly dangerous. Then it travels. From engineering to design, to legal, to finance, to marketing, each stop sanding an edge for safety. The bold experiment becomes a "phased rollout." The real-time loop becomes "post-launch optimization." The dream of reinvention becomes "efficiency improvement." Each change sounds prudent, even mature, but together they drain all heat from the idea. By the time it ships, the sentence that once felt like a revolution now reads like a press release.

The ledger records translation costs too, the hours lost reconciling dashboards that refuse to agree. Marketing's activation rate says 78%. Product says 64%. Data says 70%, "within confidence." They are all correct in isolation and all wrong in reality. Smart people spend their best hours stitching together truths that should have been born connected. They are no longer building products; they are building consensus. Alignment becomes the work itself, a ritual of making the numbers rhyme instead of the system run.

Efficiency tools, meant to speed things up, start multiplying friction. Five identity systems. Three analytics stacks. Two tax engines. A patchwork of integrations that make every improvement a negotiation. What once required code now requires diplomacy. The company still calls itself "agile," but its data moves like cold syrup. Nobody decides to make it slow; it simply becomes heavy through success.

Opportunity decay is harder to see but easier to feel. A decision deferred for one more quarter quietly reshapes the future. Standards harden, partnerships move on, competitors release what you were still refining. What was once a choice becomes an obligation, what was once an advantage becomes catch-up. Bureaucracy doesn't just slow progress, it shrinks the number of futures available.

Defects also compound in silence. A warning raised by one team dies politely in another's inbox. A bug that should take hours to fix metastasizes across systems that don't talk. By the time it surfaces as a crisis, ownership has dissolved into process. The organization pays twice: once in outage and again in reputation. The incident gets documented. The cause remains systemic.

Then come the quiet debts of maintenance. Every workaround, every pilot that never ended, every shim that made last quarter possible adds a few ounces of weight. None of it breaks the company; it simply thickens it. Engineers call it technical debt. Managers call it business as usual. Over time, the system becomes self-defending, too complex to question, too interlocked to move.

Each layer of variance, regional, legal, or contractual, multiplies the points where someone can ask a fair question that no one can answer easily. "Where is this data stored?" "Who approved this change?" "Why does it behave differently in Europe?" Every answer exists somewhere, but never in one place. The scramble to connect them costs money, yes, but costs trust first. In an age where speed and transparency are inseparable, that erosion of trust is a slow bleed no CFO can measure but every customer can feel.

As these patterns deepen, the company stops spending energy on creation and starts spending it on maintenance, of process, perception, and permission. A new clause here, a new exception there, until each initiative requires a treaty instead of a plan. People stop asking, "What's right for the customer?" and start asking, "Whose OK do we need?" Change becomes a diplomatic act.

Ritual takes over. A day a week disappears into pre-reads, steering updates, and reviews. The meetings meant to support work become the work. The dashboard that was designed to reveal progress becomes the stage where progress is performed. The company's rhythm becomes a simulation of productivity, steady, predictable, low amplitude.

And through it all, customers notice before anyone else. They feel the seams that no dashboard can see. The product still works, but it doesn't surprise. The updates still ship, but they don't matter. Trust doesn't collapse, it fades. Indifference becomes the default, and indifference is the final stage of decline. When your users stop expecting more from you, they've already moved on.

Add it all up, the lost days, the softened ideas, the duplicated effort, the friction masked as process, and the pattern emerges. Companies don't fail because they run out of money or intelligence. They fail because they accumulate drag faster than they create thrust. They stop accelerating. The visible books show stability; the hidden ledger shows decay.

Healthy organizations don't just balance their budgets; they manage entropy. They reclaim energy lost to translation, delay, and fear. They measure what others ignore, the time between decision and action, the number of approvals per change, the distance between customer signal and shipped response. These are not operational trivia. They are early warnings, the vital signs of a company's ability to move.

The hidden ledger exists in every organization. Most ignore it until the market audits it for them, a competitor releases what they almost built, a talent wave leaves for places that move faster, a once-loyal customer chooses someone more alive. By then, the numbers still look fine. But the slope, the true indicator of life, has flattened.

You can't close the ledger by decree or by dashboard. You close it by design, by giving someone ownership of the seams, by aligning clocks across the walls, by trading local green for global momentum. That's how companies learn to conduct energy again.

Every leader eventually discovers the hidden ledger. The only difference is when, while they still have time to change the slope, or after the slope has already changed them.

Leadership by Perimeter

Every ledger has an author, even the hidden one. The signatures may not appear on paper, but they live in the design of authority, in how power is distributed, how decisions are made, and how accountability is drawn. The pattern is as familiar as it is fatal: the higher an organization rises, the narrower each leader's horizon becomes. Clarity replaces curiosity. Command replaces connection. And the company begins to run on perimeter power, leadership that governs the edges while leaving the center hollow.

At first, it looks like excellence. Each executive owns a clean domain: Product, Marketing, Sales, Operations, Finance, Legal, Security, Regions. Their dashboards are immaculate; their teams are disciplined. The Monday staff meeting looks like a triumph of order, one fortress after another reporting strength. Numbers rise on cue, risks are "bounded," dependencies are "under management." It feels like control. It's really choreography. The room applauds coordination, but no one owns the corridors between the forts.

Perimeter leadership thrives on clarity because clarity protects careers. Inside the fence, you can measure everything, ROI, retention, forecast accuracy, compliance incidents. Outside it, in the messy middle where disciplines collide, metrics blur, ownership diffuses, and risk multiplies. So leaders retreat to the ground they can defend, not the ground the company needs them to explore. The seams become no one's jurisdiction. The company begins to rot at the joints.

The tells are subtle. Slides that travel horizontally across departments arrive with a "dependency" box instead of a decision. The most important diagrams have footnotes longer than the content. Words like "alignment," "resource constraints," and "phase two" become polite ways of saying, *we know what's right, but no one owns the risk to do it.* Leaders leave meetings relieved when their perimeter stayed intact, not concerned that the corridor stayed empty.

Budget season turns this geometry into policy. Each department defends its map of the world with color-coded precision, complete with a spreadsheet that proves ROI within its borders. The initiatives that require two budgets, three calendars, and shared downside arrive last. They are shaved down to pilots, postponed to next year, or absorbed under "strategic review." The spreadsheet balances. The future doesn't.

Escalations reveal the same physics in reverse. A customer issue that touches multiple functions climbs up the chain, collecting VPs along the way, until it lands in the CEO's inbox as a false binary: pick a fence to breach. The fix that would require crossing budgets, rewriting a contract, or denting a quarterly metric is framed as "too disruptive right now." A workaround is blessed. The ticket closes green. The defect reproduces.

The most dangerous thing about perimeter leadership is that it looks responsible. A Sales VP who tightens forecast discipline is prudent. A Security head who slows deployment for review is careful. A Finance chief who protects margin optics is rational. Every act of caution makes sense in isolation. Together, they form a ring of reason that keeps the organization safe from exactly the kind of friction it needs to grow.

Even data bends to this geometry. Dashboards evolve to measure what each leader can move directly. Anything that requires collaboration becomes a proxy metric or a narrative. Over time, the company becomes exquisitely precise about the wrong things. Revenue by SKU, uptime by service, NPS by region, all clean, all contained, all technically true. But the numbers that live in the corridors, time from idea to shipped outcome, decisions requiring multiple approvals, forks in core processes, never make the first slide. What isn't measured by a perimeter doesn't survive a quarter.

People adapt to the terrain. Directors learn to bring "clean" asks that fit inside one budget, one calendar, one KPI. PMs learn to pre-trim scope to survive the gauntlet of approvals, labeling the rest "phase two." Counsel learns to say "supportive in principle" when the contract doesn't yet exist. Engineering learns to code adapters and shims faster than the organization can negotiate alignment. None of it is malicious. It's muscle memory in a system where survival means staying legible.

Eventually, this way of leading becomes the culture. Teams no longer ask, "What's the right thing for the company?" They ask, "Whose metric does this move?" Leaders stop trading local green for global gain. They stop taking bets that might disturb the surface of calm. The company starts looking more like a coalition of fiefdoms than a single organism. Strategy becomes a series of overlapping speeches that share vocabulary but not velocity.

Every now and then, a crisis breaks the choreography. A product fails publicly, a customer churns dramatically, a regulator asks a question the company can't answer cleanly. For a few weeks, the walls collapse. Decision-making becomes fluid again. Budgets bend. Hierarchies flatten. The company remembers what speed feels like. The results are stunning, fixes that once seemed impossible happen in days. Everyone calls it "the war room effect." And then, just as quickly, the old walls rebuild. The forts resume their posts. The war room dissolves back into a calendar invite.

The lesson never sticks because the system rewards control, not motion. Leaders who protect their domains are promoted. Leaders who breach boundaries are tolerated once, then sidelined for "creating turbulence." The organization keeps its balance sheet spotless and its imagination impoverished. It is led by caretakers of the known.

But there's another kind of leadership, one that refuses to live by perimeter. These leaders understand that the seams are where advantage hides. They walk the corridors, not the walls. They listen for the frictions that dashboards don't capture. They trade short-term optics for long-term motion. They don't punish ambiguity; they harvest it. They measure their success not by how stable their departments feel, but by how much faster the organization learns.

Companies that rediscover motion do so not because they redesigned their structure, but because they redefined leadership. They give someone authority over the in-between, the right to trade local success for global coherence, the mandate to align clocks and collapse forks. They institutionalize the ability to make diagonal decisions. They make motion someone's job.

Until that happens, the company will keep performing competence without progress. It will keep managing the perimeter while the middle grows quiet. The ledger will keep expanding, invisible but exacting, charging interest on every decision that could have crossed a border but didn't.

Leadership by perimeter is not leadership at all, it's administration of the past. The leaders who will define the next decade are the ones willing to lead across the seams, not just within them. The future belongs to those who can hold the whole system in their hands and still move.

Case Studies: The Cost of Distance

1. Disney: The Bundle That Couldn't Connect

In 2019, Disney made a bold promise: one seamless streaming experience that united Disney+, Hulu, and ESPN+ under a single digital roof. The idea was sound, a family-friendly platform that could serve every audience from toddlers to sports fans. But behind that promise was a structure that made "seamless" nearly impossible.

Each service had been built as its own company, with its own teams, infrastructure, and incentives. Disney+ was an engineering-driven product optimized for subscription growth. Hulu was a legacy content platform run by broadcast veterans focused on ad revenue and licensing rights. ESPN+ lived under an entirely different technology stack and compliance regime. From day one, integration meant crossing not just codebases but cultures.

Marketing led the charge, announcing a unified "Disney Bundle" that would launch in 2021. Engineering cautioned that the systems weren't ready; finance wanted a shared billing system before consolidation; legal raised red flags over overlapping content rights. The project moved anyway, in parts.

By late 2022, internal reports showed over 120 integration dependencies across divisions. Each milestone depended on three approvals, each approval on a team with different success metrics. Logins broke, ad inventory misaligned, and personalization algorithms failed to share user data across platforms. A single household could hold three separate user IDs tied to one credit card, one for each service.

Customers noticed. Complaints about "bundle confusion" spiked; support tickets increased by 40% during the 2023 rebranding rollout. The cost wasn't just reputational, ad targeting errors and licensing delays were estimated to have erased $350 million in revenue. Engineers joked that "the bundle works better in marketing slides than in code."

But the deeper story was structural. The bundle wasn't failing because teams were incompetent, they were excellent at what they owned. It failed because no one owned the space between. Marketing owned the narrative. Engineering owned the platform. Legal owned the rights. No one owned the experience.

Disney eventually solved the technical problem, a shared ID spine and unified analytics layer, but the organizational repair came later. Leadership had to rewrite incentives to reward cross-division coherence, not just division-level performance. It wasn't a software fix; it was a systems fix.

The bundle finally began to work. Not because the code got smarter, but because the company did.

2. Meta: Velocity Without Vision

Few companies move faster than Meta. In its engineering corridors, speed is gospel, the company's mantra, "move fast," is practically engraved in its source code. Yet by 2023, Meta's biggest challenge wasn't speed; it was coherence. The company had built an innovation engine that produced motion without momentum.

The core problem wasn't technical; it was architectural. Product teams operated like semi-autonomous startups, each with its own metrics, roadmaps, and review processes. Instagram optimized for creator engagement, Facebook for retention, WhatsApp for trust and uptime, and Reality Labs for hardware adoption. The result was a company accelerating in four directions at once.

At one point, over 800 concurrent experiments were live across Meta's platforms. Engineering celebrated the throughput, new releases shipped daily, some twice a day. But the system had no shared governor, no unifying principle to connect these bursts of activity into a coherent experience.

When a privacy rework launched on Facebook in late 2022, the data schema used to track user permissions diverged subtly from Instagram's by just two fields. That minor mismatch created cascading issues: analytics dashboards drifted, ad conversion metrics split, and reporting pipelines desynchronized. For six months, the same campaign could show three different ROI numbers depending on which app's backend was queried.

Meanwhile, design and UX teams struggled with divergence. Button styles, gesture responses, even content sorting logic began to differ between Meta apps. Support tickets citing "confusing app behavior" rose 27% year over year, while engagement per session flattened despite feature proliferation. Meta wasn't suffering from too few ideas, it was drowning in them.

Executives began to realize that the fragmentation wasn't cultural noise; it was systemic feedback. Each team's definition of success was locally rational but globally incoherent. The platform had stopped learning as one organism.

In response, Meta launched the "Integrity Mesh" initiative, an internal attempt to unify decision-making data across all apps. It reduced redundant metrics by 42% and established a single data governance model for ads and privacy. But even that reform underscored the root issue: for years, truth itself had been fragmented.

Meta's story isn't one of incompetence, but of physics. When too many teams run at maximum velocity without a shared compass, entropy wins. The seams between functions become the real product, and users feel every one.

3. Pfizer & Moderna: Speed Through Alignment

In early 2020, as a global pandemic halted industries and economies, two companies faced an impossible challenge: develop, test, manufacture, and distribute an entirely new class of vaccine, mRNA-based, in record time. What followed wasn't a miracle of science alone; it was a triumph of organizational design.

Moderna, then a mid-sized biotech with around 1,000 employees, built its COVID-19 vaccine by treating its data infrastructure as a living nervous system. Clinical teams, bioinformatics, and manufacturing all fed into a single cloud platform, every trial result, every assay, every batch run updated in real time. Regulatory liaisons had direct dashboard access, eliminating the lag between experiment and approval.

The result was astonishing: Moderna went from genetic sequencing of the virus to its first human dose in 63 days. Not because it had more people, but because the people it had were connected by one system that didn't lose time in translation.

Pfizer, a behemoth 20 times larger, faced a harder challenge, scale and bureaucracy. Historically, a single vaccine program might take 8–10 years, slowed by committees, review cycles, and departmental silos. But for its COVID-19 response, leadership created an internal startup: Project Lightspeed.

Lightspeed had sovereign authority. It bypassed three layers of management, unified 250 staff across R&D, regulatory, supply chain, and legal, and collapsed decision time from weeks to hours. Every cross-functional meeting was daily; every dependency visible in one integrated tracker.

By compressing feedback loops, Pfizer reduced the time from initial design to FDA authorization to under 300 days, an order-of-magnitude acceleration unmatched in modern pharmaceutical history. Manufacturing scaled globally in parallel with trials, using predictive logistics models that simulated bottlenecks weeks in advance.

The measurable outcome: more than 3 billion doses distributed within two years, billions of lives impacted, and an enduring case study in what happens when bureaucracy yields to coherence.

Pfizer and Moderna proved that scale and speed can coexist, but only when information flows freely and decisions live closest to reality. Their systems didn't just move fast; they moved together.

The Pattern Beneath the Stories

Across industries, the architecture of failure looks eerily similar. Whether it's streaming platforms, social networks, or pharmaceutical giants, the enemy isn't incompetence, it's misalignment. Innovation doesn't collapse in a single moment; it erodes quietly, through translation, delay, and good intentions stretched across too many boundaries.

At Disney, the walls were vertical. Each division was a model of excellence, marketing, engineering, content licensing, all performing brilliantly inside their own lanes. Yet together they produced dissonance. The product that was meant to unify families fragmented them instead, one login screen at a time. The code wasn't broken; the company was divided by design.

At Meta, the walls ran horizontally. Teams sprinted at full velocity, but in different directions. The platform became a chorus of brilliant solos, Instagram perfecting engagement, Facebook refining retention, Reality Labs chasing the horizon of the metaverse, each playing louder to be heard, until the melody of the company vanished under the noise. The tragedy wasn't stagnation; it was entropy disguised as progress.

And then came Pfizer and Moderna, two organizations that faced chaos and refused to move separately. Where others built committees, they built corridors. Where others wrote approvals, they wrote code. In less than a year, they turned science into salvation not through speed alone, but through synchronization. When the world stopped, they moved as one.

What these stories reveal is that innovation isn't lost in failure; it's lost in translation. When truth moves slowly, time stretches. When ownership fragments, momentum evaporates. When success is measured in parts, the whole stops learning.

Disney's fragmentation cost coherence. Meta's acceleration cost direction. Pfizer and Moderna's alignment bought time, and in a world of exponential change, time is the only real currency.

The geometry of motion determines destiny. Companies that master synchronization turn complexity into rhythm. Those that don't, no matter how vast or brilliant, eventually fall out of tune.

But silos aren't built by engineers alone, they're reinforced by leaders. The fractures that begin as distance between teams harden into policies, budgets, and incentives. The same logic that fragments a codebase fragments an executive team. The dashboard that reports green hides the corridor that's turning gray.

The next layer of the problem isn't operational; it's political. Leadership itself becomes a set of verticals, each fortified, each fluent in its own truth. Coordination turns into performance, collaboration into ceremony. The company doesn't just lose speed; it loses a shared sense of direction.

And that's where the story turns next, from the friction between functions to the geometry of power. Because once the seams climb into the boardroom, the problem changes shape. It's no longer about systems that can't talk to each other; it's about leaders who won't.

Conclusion: The Cost of Distance

Every company believes it's connected, until it tries to move. From the inside, the seams between teams feel like structure, accountability, maturity. From the outside, they look like friction, time that doesn't add up, ideas that die between approvals, customers who feel the lag before anyone else does.

Silos don't announce themselves. They form in the quiet moments when coordination feels slower than autonomy, when "alignment" becomes shorthand for delay, when protecting one's lane feels safer than crossing it. Over time, these choices harden into architecture. The company that once built products begins to build process instead.

In the beginning, every organization has one clock, the customer's. As it grows, new clocks appear: engineering's cadence, marketing's calendar, finance's quarter, compliance's review. Each one ticks rationally on its own, but together they desynchronize. Time stretches. Urgency diffuses. The future slips between cycles that no longer meet.

You can see it in dashboards that glow green while the slope stays flat. In meetings where no one lies but everyone edits the truth. In post-mortems that read like success stories with missing verbs. The most expensive losses aren't visible in revenue, they live in translation, in the hours between versions of the same idea.

And yet, the same pattern that kills innovation can also resurrect it. Alignment is not the opposite of speed; it's the foundation for it. When distance collapses, when engineering and marketing share one definition of success, when data and design see the same user, when

155

leadership measures progress by learning, not optics, momentum returns almost instantly.

Pfizer and Moderna showed that connection at scale is not a dream; it's design. Meta proved that motion without coherence burns energy instead of creating it. Disney's tangle revealed that beauty inside the walls means little if the corridors stay dark.

The lesson is as simple as it is hard: innovation lives in the spaces between functions. When those spaces belong to no one, progress leaks. When someone owns them, with budget, authority, and the courage to trade local green bars for global movement, a company can breathe again.

There are no villains in this story, only systems that forget their rhythm. The cure is not more meetings, but more conductivity, fewer walls, clearer truths, faster loops. Because every organization, no matter how slow it has become, still remembers the pulse it started with.

What matters is whether it can hear it again.

When systems stall, it's rarely because of ignorance or malice. It's fear, fear of failure, fear of scrutiny, fear of losing what's already been earned. Once fear becomes the quiet governor of decision-making, speed turns into caution, and caution calcifies into culture. The next chapter begins there: where the walls aren't built from structure or process, but from psychology, how organizations mistake safety for stewardship, and how rebuilding a bias for decisive, reversible bets can restore not just momentum, but courage.

CHAPTER 6

Risk Aversion and the Fear of Failure

The Preference for Certainty

It begins as good housekeeping. Forecasts tighten, guidance gets specific, and the organization learns the comfort of hitting what it promises. Reliability turns into a kind of internal currency: the leaders who "never miss" get more rope, more budget, more trust. Soon the planning ritual flips the logic. We don't forecast what we will do; we back-solve what we can safely say. The roadmap trims its own edges until the confidence interval looks respectable in a board deck.

Finance quietly codifies the instinct. Variance is treated as defect, not discovery. Sensitivity analyses that should surface upside and downside are used to sand them off. The models reward explainable outcomes over valuable ones, so proposals arrive pre-sanitized: smaller scope, fewer unknowns, tighter ranges. The spreadsheet approves the plan; the plan approves the spreadsheet.

Narrative risk eclipses product risk. The hardest part of a bold bet isn't building it, it's explaining it before it works. "Disciplined focus" is easier to defend than "uncomfortable maybe," so the selection pressure favors stories that land neatly. We start choosing initiatives we can narrate instead of those that could move the curve. The vocabulary changes first: from "what if" to "what we can commit."

The portfolio clamps around the middle. Stage-gates, hurdle rates, and review councils converge on outcomes that look prudent on paper: no disasters, no breakthroughs, a tight cluster around plan. Outliers, good and bad, are engineered out. It feels like professionalism. It behaves like stagnation.

The calendar becomes a safety device. Reviews multiply to "de-risk," launches drift to friendlier quarters, dependencies are phased so each team can preserve its on-time record. Speed doesn't die in engineering; it dies in scheduling. We call it sequencing and feel responsible while momentum drains away.

Metrics migrate toward stability. We stop arguing about p95 and start reporting "incident-free days." We replace time-to-adoption with "launch completeness." Numbers that move slowly are safer to promise, so we optimize the slow ones. The dashboards look calm; the market doesn't.

The core business sets unspoken guardrails. New things must not dent channels, partners, or lines that pay the bills. Disruptive ideas are resized into "adjacencies" that won't offend the present. Legal and vendor contracts harden that posture: clauses to avoid edge cases multiply, export paths narrow, and changing anything starts to require diplomacy. When progress needs permission, continuity wins.

People read the room. Builders feel the air thin and take their variance elsewhere. Maintainers inherit the machinery and run it well. Quality persists. Surprise vanishes. The company becomes excellent at producing what it can predict, and quietly trades tomorrow's slope for today's smooth line.

How Fear Enters the Org Chart

It starts above the org chart, with the audience that never ships anything: boards and markets. Guidance becomes a promise, and the cost of a miss isn't just financial, it's narrative. Directors ask for "line of sight," analysts for "consistency," and the system discovers that the easiest way to deliver both is to take fewer surprises. From there, plans aren't chosen for expected value but for explainability. Optionality is shaved until outcomes cluster.

The CEO/CFO layer turns variance into story. A bet is no longer judged only by its potential, but by how it will read in a letter and on a call. Calendar math, what lands before earnings, quietly outranks compounding math, what bends the curve after earnings. "De-risk" shifts meaning: not guardrails around a bold plan, but scope reductions until the plan is safe to narrate.

General managers inherit the posture as custodians of lines. Their job is run-rate health: tidy funnels, predictable unit economics, partner peace. Anything that threatens today's denominator, channel, attach, ASP, must arrive "adjacent." Cannibalization becomes a reputational hazard, so disruptive ideas are resized to fit the frame. The portfolio fills with projects that make sense and change little.

Middle management becomes the translation zone where ambition is resized to survive. Promotion math rewards error-free delivery; review math punishes visible misses. Managers pre-trim proposals to clear three committees, rename risk "phase one," turn learning into "post-launch." Success becomes the absence of surprises between QBRs. The unseen cost is momentum.

Program and project offices absorb uncertainty and sell back certainty as process. Stage gates multiply, templates harden, risk registers expand until they capture only what's already known. Schedules synchronize to governance cycles, not customers. Speed doesn't die in engineering; it dies in waiting rooms.

Legal, risk, and compliance arrive as brakes and become rails. Vague mandates, avoid "undue exposure", travel faster than explicit allowances. Where policy is ambiguous, defaults trend to no or "not this quarter." Contracts collect "for safety" clauses that read well and quietly remove degrees of freedom. When progress requires diplomacy, continuity wins.

Security and privacy amplify the caution. Breach optics begin to outweigh breach probability. Controls are written to neutralize edge cases; exceptions feel existential. Teams design for audit rather than impact. The most honest documents move to private drives.

Compensation calcifies the posture. Bonuses tie to on-time delivery and incident-free quarters, not learning velocity or asymmetric upside. Calibration celebrates reliability as a leadership trait. High-variance performers peak unless their variance has already paid off. The culture rebalances around maintainers who never scare anyone.

Product management curates backlogs for narratability. Items with clear effort/benefit get greenlit; asymmetric bets with messy measurement are deferred as "needs research." Roadmaps optimize for stakeholder comfort. Exploration is quarantined off-slide so it won't invite unanswerable questions. The map gets smoother; the terrain doesn't.

Engineering shifts its definition of done from *solved the problem* to *met the gate*. Debt labeled "risk" is deferred; shims ship because they're easier to explain. Architecture favors reversibility over potential. Senior ICs learn that the fastest path to a strong rating is incident avoidance, not ceiling-raising.

Design and research are pulled from discovery toward validation. Briefs stop asking "what could this be?" and start asking "prove this won't fail." Studies overfit to de-risk decisions already made. Bold patterns live as "experiments" that never see production.

Data and analytics smooth the optics. Metrics drift toward those least likely to embarrass: "launch completeness" over adoption time, "incident-free days" over p95 reality. Dashboards stabilize, comparables look clean, and analysts spend their best hours reconciling truths rather than surfacing uncomfortable ones. The picture improves; the product doesn't.

Vendors and partnerships lock the posture into place. Third parties are chosen for headline safety over leverage. SLAs and indemnities look immaculate while export paths narrow and exit clauses vanish. The cheapest short-term route hardens long-term constraints. When a breakthrough needs a different clause, it's "too late in the cycle."

You can see the residue in artifacts without a bulleted list: roadmaps with quarters of medium bets and no spikes; business cases with tight ranges and immaculate footnotes; risk logs where the biggest risks are presentation, not product; OKRs that read like service-level promises. Meetings tilt the same way, questions drift from "does it work?" to "who owns it?" to "how will it look?", and decisions migrate to the option that's most reversible.

Nothing breaks. That's the point. Fear doesn't slam doors; it pads the hallway. The organization learns to exchange upside variance for narrative control, and it feels like maturity. But the curve flattens, the option set narrows, and the company becomes the best version of itself, yesterday.

The Corporate Immune System

It doesn't say "no." It says "route through the proper channel." The first time you try something unfamiliar, the organization responds like a body sensing foreign matter: it surrounds the idea with forms, wraps it in reviews, and isolates it in a safe place where it can't touch anything vital. Not malicious, protective. The purpose is continuity. The effect is quarantine.

The antibodies have names: risk council, architecture review, brand safety, data governance, partner operations, privacy, security, regional compliance, PMO. Each does its job well in isolation. Together they perform pattern matching on yesterday's failures and apply the remedy to tomorrow's ideas. A feature that crosses two data boundaries triggers privacy, then security, then legal, then vendor contracts. By the time it returns, the feature is smaller, later, and less connected to the thing it was meant to change.

Process turns uncertainty into paperwork. Templates ask questions you can only answer after you've learned something; the learning can't begin until the template is complete. Exceptions exist, but the exception path is a maze with tasteful signage. You get an exception for this quarter, then an extension for the pilot, then a reminder that exceptions can't be permanent. The immune system wins by exhausting momentum.

Committees are calibrated for the last incident. A fraud spike hardens KYC to the point where onboarding becomes attrition. A brand flare-up expands review scopes until copy ships late and timid. A supplier miss adds three new approvals to every purchase order. Scar tissue reads as maturity: controls that never relax because the memory of pain outlives the cause. The new idea pays rent on injuries it didn't cause.

When the organism can't kill novelty outright, it encapsulates it. That's what "innovation labs," "sandboxes," and "pilots" become when misused: containment zones. The badge opens a different door, the sprint board runs on a different cadence, the demo is applauded, and the interface to the core is a presentation, not a bus. Graduation requires adapters no one funded and risk owners no one named. The lab thrives. The company doesn't change.

Metrics adapt to the immune response. Success is redefined as "no escalation," "no audit findings," "no severity-ones." Slides show incident-free days while customer patience decays. Post-mortems conclude with new checks more often than with fewer steps. The number of gates increases quarter over quarter; cycle time to permission exceeds cycle time to build. Everyone can prove they improved safety. No one can prove they improved outcomes.

Vendors and contracts supply the low-level proteins. Boilerplate terms, no export, no derivative modeling, no benchmark disclosure, are sold as prudence and priced as permanent constraint. The cheapest short-term SLA becomes the most expensive long-term architecture. When a breakthrough requires a different clause, procurement calls it "off-template" and schedules the next quarter.

People adapt their behavior to survive the antibodies. Product rewrites briefs to fit the template; design moves discovery into "research that confirms"; engineering substitutes shims for structural change because shims pass review. Risk teams, overwhelmed by volume, raise the threshold for attention until only the scariest proposals get a human yes or no. Everything else waits. Waiting teaches caution better than policy ever could.

The immune system scales with success. A good quarter funds more protection: new policies, fresh dashboards, broader gates. Each control felt reasonable when introduced; collectively they become the operating system. Leaders inherit a climate where removing a guardrail feels reckless, adding one feels responsible. No one earns a bonus for the step they safely deleted.

You can diagnose the posture without a forensic audit. Count pilots that never graduated. Measure approval latency against build latency. Track the ratio of post-mortem actions that add checks versus those that remove them. Look for exception committees that meet more often than launch committees. If the organization spends more time proving it is safe than proving it is right, the immune system is in charge.

Nothing here is villainy. The system is doing what it was designed to do: keep the organism alive. But protection without renewal becomes self-harm. The corporate immune system preserves the body by preventing adaptation. It converts discovery into documentation, replaces risk with ritual, and lets the company die in a state of perfect health, on paper. How to keep the antibodies and regain the nerve belongs to the next chapter.

The Mechanics of Caution

Caution doesn't arrive with a policy memo; it seeps in through the fittings. Forecast reviews start to prefer tight ranges over big outcomes, so proposals show up already shrunk to fit the frame. What should be a choice between expected value and explainability becomes a choice between comfort and risk, and comfort wins. The variance gets filtered out first in spreadsheets, then in roadmaps, then in people. Big swings aren't rejected; they're resized until they can't move the curve.

Time turns into a safety device. Launches slide to friendlier quarters, cross-team dependencies are "sequenced," and meetings proliferate to "de-risk" what might have shipped. Speed doesn't die in the code; it dies in calendars. Stage gates multiply with good reasons attached to each, but in sequence they convert uncertainty into ceremony. The path of least resistance becomes the path of most reversibility. By the time an initiative clears the gauntlet, it's the version easiest to undo, not the one most worth doing.

Narrative begins to outrank product. The question shifts from *Will this bend the slope?* to *Can we defend this on the call?* Metrics follow suit. p95 latency becomes "incident-free days," adoption becomes "launch completeness," learning velocity becomes "on-time delivery." Dashboards calm down while customers don't. The company starts optimizing numbers that move slowly because slow numbers are safer to promise.

Guardrails tighten around the core. New ideas are invited in on the condition that they won't dent channels, partners, or the line that pays the bills. Legal and procurement harden that posture into contracts: clauses that read like prudence and spend like permanence.

When progress needs a different term, it's "off-template" and "next quarter." Teams learn to ship shims instead of spine, adapters that pass review today and compound complexity tomorrow. The architecture grows polite and heavy.

Experiments are allowed as long as they remain small. Pilots proliferate, each called a success, none given a bridge to production. Graduation requires owners and budgets that were never named. Meanwhile, risk registers fill with presentation hazards, stakeholder confusion, brand ambiguity, while the product risks that matter are managed by delay. Post-mortems conclude with more checks, rarely with fewer steps. Scar tissue becomes policy.

Conversation changes temperature. Decisions migrate to pre-reads where edges are sanded before the meeting. In the room, live options reduce to the least controversial one. The phrases multiply, "phase it," "pilot first," "after peak," "not this quarter", and nobody needs to say no because the calendar says it for them. Analysts spend Thursdays reconciling truths across silos so the story will match itself. The picture improves; the product doesn't.

Taken together, this is how caution works: not as a dramatic veto, but as a steady exchange of upside variance for narrative control. The machine hits its marks and misses its moment. Releases arrive precisely when the window has narrowed, meticulously prepared for a world that has moved on. The lines on the slide look smooth. The slope in reality goes flat.

Example: Intel: from roadmap to risk management

The breaking point was public. In July 2020, Intel admitted its 7nm (later "Intel 4") was late due to yield issues, a headline slip that triggered leadership churn and a visible retreat into "explainable" deliverables. The message to planners became: avoid another surprise. Roadmaps were resized, windows padded, guidance sanded to fit optics.

While Intel filtered variance out of its plans, AMD leaned into it, riding TSMC's leading nodes and taking share in the highest-mix segments. By Q2-2025, Mercury Research data showed ~27.3% server CPU units for AMD and ~41% of server CPU revenue, with desktop unit share at ~32.2%. Those are the compounding dividends of tolerating near-term volatility to win premium mix, while the incumbent managed downside.

Fear shaped capital bets too. Intel's effort to reassert foundry scale (IDM 2.0) needed bold, time-certain execution; instead, flagship pieces slipped into "when the timing is right." The Ohio fab complex, once pitched for mid-decade output, slid to 2030–2031 for the first plant, with the second to 2032, a timeline that reads prudent to investors but translates to forfeited learning cycles in manufacturing and customer design-ins.

Inside any large chipmaker, some caution is rational (nobody wants another node miss). But after a public failure, the *denominator* of acceptable risk shrinks. Review boards proliferate; targets skew to what can be met rather than what must be won. The measurable result is portfolio convergence on reversible steps, safe steppings, conservative customer ramps, incremental core counts, while rivals cash in the upside of being first when it matters. Intel's recent counterpunches (Xeon 6, client refreshes) may claw back ground, but the tax of five years of "don't-miss" planning shows up in market mix, not just headlines.

Takeaway: once failure becomes a public narrative, organizations often optimize to avoid the next headline rather than to maximize the next inflection. The cost posts later, as share, margins, and time.

Example: Apple: Project Titan and the decade of "don't ship wrong"

Apple's car wasn't undone by lack of money or talent, it was undone by a rising bar for what could be safely revealed without scarring the brand. Over nearly a decade, the program cycled ambitions (Level-5 autonomy to more modest ADAS) while headcount and spend mounted. In Feb 2024, Apple formally canceled the effort, reassigning roughly 2,000 people; reporting pegs the cumulative investment at >$10 billion.

The fear mechanism here is subtler than "we were scared to build a car." It's the brand's intolerance for visible misses. Each leadership review pushed the threshold higher: if autonomy isn't magic, if manufacturing isn't seamless, if service isn't Apple-grade on day one, then wait. That posture protects reputation, but it also converts a moving market into an eligibility test you can never quite pass. Meanwhile, EV unit economics shifted, autonomy timelines elongated, capital costs rose, and the competitive field consolidated. By the time caution felt fully justified, the opportunity surface had thinned.

Quantitatively, the opportunity cost looks like this: a decade of engineering burn at ~$1B+/year (press estimates) with no deployed fleet, no learning miles, and no supplier leverage that comes from shipping at scale. Even the endgame was optics-aware, the team pivoted to generative AI (a safer, brand-aligned narrative with nearer-term wins) and trimmed staff, rather than hard-launch a compromised vehicle that might haunt the halo.

Takeaway: when a company defines "failure" as a public blemish rather than a private learning loop, it drifts toward indefinite readiness. The result is perfect caution and zero compounding.

What Fear Produces (you can measure it)

You don't need a manifesto to know fear is running the place; the clocks and dashboards confess it. The first tell is time itself. Work that takes three weeks to build now spends five to seven weeks in pre-reads, gates, risk councils, and "alignment." Decision latency becomes the real critical path. Roadmaps start following the meeting calendar rather than the market window, and shipping quietly turns into scheduling.

Variance flattens next. Portfolio reviews used to have spikes, two big, scary bets surrounded by sensible work. Then the spikes disappear. Forecasts hit within a neat ±3%, quarter after quarter, while the outside world swings wildly. Internally, this looks like maturity. Externally, market share drifts a half point at a time. Tight variance in a noisy environment is not control; it's self-editing.

Pilots multiply like souvenirs. Every quarter produces a fresh crop of "successful experiments," and yet the production graph barely moves. Graduation stretches from two quarters to four, then to "not this fiscal." The museum gets bigger: plaques, demos, learning documents. The core business remains unchanged. When you plot it, the pilot-to-production ratio climbs; the line that matters does not.

Reversibility takes the wheel. In meetings, the winner is the option that's easiest to undo, not the one most worth doing. Commit memos pivot from "highest expected value" to "lowest risk of regret." The portfolio becomes a garden of reversible decisions, three or five to every one consequential call. Nothing terrible happens. Nothing compounding does, either.

The calendar becomes a shield. Launches bunch up against optics windows, the fortnight before earnings, the keynote week, the partner summit, because visibility is a risk to be managed. Slips are renamed "sequencing." Release heatmaps glow around investor dates rather than customer need. It reads like orchestration. It feels like hiding.

Metrics drift into comfort. Dashboards trade outcomes for optics: p95 latency becomes "incident-free days," adoption turns into "launch completeness," learning velocity is rebadged as "on-time delivery." Scorecards get greener while users grumble the same. When leaders ask "How are we doing?" the graphs answer "stable," and the business answers "slower."

Risk logs change species. The top entries used to say "fails under load," "model bias at edge cases," "supplier single-point." Now they say "stakeholder confusion," "brand ambiguity," "messaging misalignment." Post-mortems end with more checks than removals; scar tissue becomes policy. Each new control was reasonable on its own. Together they become the operating system.

Money tilts backward. Budgets settle into the known: maintenance creeps from 50% of engineering hours to 60, then 70, while exploration shrinks to what can be promised in a quarter. R&D as a share of revenue holds flat, but enablement headcount rises. Funding rounds for hard problems demand proof that only shipping can provide, so teams resize proposals to fit the ask. Ambition survives as a deck.

Contracts harden, then harden again. Procurement templates accrete "safe" clauses, no export, no derivative modeling, strict SLAs, until every new partner looks the same. Exceptions require two signatures last year, three this year. Optionality decays in legalese. The cheapest SLA today becomes the most expensive architecture tomorrow.

Discovery gives way to validation. Research hours migrate from "What could this be?" to "Prove this won't fail." Bold patterns get quarantined in experiments that never graduate. Design is asked for reassurance, not direction. The ratio of discovery to validation slides down each quarter, and with it the surface area where something genuinely new might appear.

Even the architecture tells on itself. Instead of refactoring spine, teams layer shims and feature flags that pass review today and compound drag tomorrow. Incidents don't spike, operational friction does. The system grows polite and heavy. Engineers spend more time reconciling truths across systems than changing the truth for customers.

Listen closely and the language confirms what the numbers implied. "Phase it." "Pilot first." "After peak." "Not this quarter." Decisions migrate to pre-reads where edges are sanded down before anyone meets, and the room convenes to ratify the least controversial option. Silence does the rest.

If you insist on a diagnosis, you don't need philosophy, just ratios. When days to permission exceed days to build, when internal variance is tighter than external conditions, when more pilots succeed than products ship, when launches cluster at optics windows, when post-mortems add steps and never remove them, you're not managing risk; you're manufacturing certainty. Fear has become policy, and the curve has gone flat long before the revenue line admits it.

Why It Feels Rational

Because the arguments for caution are always better dressed. In the room, the downside is concrete, regulatory letters, recall headlines, missed guidance. The upside is abstract, curves that might bend, customers who might come. Losses have names and dates; wins have hypotheticals. So the spreadsheet that caps variance reads like stewardship, and the deck that asks for slack reads like hope. No one gets fired for choosing the risk they can narrate.

Executives live inside exposure math. A single ugly quarter can cascade into analyst downgrades, board "confidence" conversations, comp compaction, and recruiting drag. A quiet upside rarely triggers a bonus you can keep; a loud downside can cost you the job you have. In that payoff table, prudence dominates. The system doesn't need a memo to become conservative, expected value loses to explainability by default.

Middle management has its own calculus. Reviews reward reliability; promotions are built on clean deliveries, not interesting scars. If a big bet works, credit diffuses. If it fails, accountability is specific. The safest way to be "top bucket" is to ship work that matches the plan and avoid surprises between QBRs. Ambition gets resized to fit the calibration grid. It feels professional because the metrics turn green.

Process adds a moral sheen. Stage gates and risk councils promise fairness and repeatability, virtues no one wants to argue against. Each new check has a story, a past sting that this control would have softened. Scar tissue becomes policy precisely because it is evidence-based. Removing steps feels like tempting fate; adding them feels like learning. The logic is internally consistent even as it pushes the organization toward ritual.

Metrics collude without meaning to. Comfort KPIs are stable and therefore "trustworthy"; outcome KPIs swing and therefore "need more context." Replace adoption with "launch completeness," p95 with "incident-free days," learning velocity with "on-time delivery," and the dashboard looks healthier every quarter. When numbers stop arguing with you, it's easy to believe the strategy is working. Smooth lines anesthetize doubt.

Legal, privacy, and security amplify the effect with asymmetric optics. A breach, a consent decree, a safety incident, these are televised. The absence of those events is invisible. Controls that eliminate tail risk feel like duty, while choices that create upside variance feel elective. Over time, "Do we need this to avoid harm?" eclipses "Do we need this to create value?" The answer to the first is usually yes; the second can always wait a quarter.

Even customers can be weaponized by caution. A handful of loud complaints can outweigh silent delight because support tickets are countable and affection isn't. Sliding the launch to "get it right" reads as customer obsession; shipping and iterating reads as impatience. When feedback loops privilege pain signals over pull signals, delay feels like empathy.

And the stories we tell ourselves seal it. Case studies of failures are forensic and vivid; case studies of bold bets that paid off are tidy and inevitable in hindsight. Survivorship bias paints pioneers as inevitabilities instead of coin flips that happened to land. So the team convinces itself that restraint is strategy, responsible, mature, investor-grade. It is not cowardice; it is craft.

That's why fear wears a suit of reason. Every small choice can be defended, every control has a receipt, every slip is "sequencing." It feels rational because at each step it is rational for someone. Only in aggregate does the posture betray its cost: a portfolio optimized for not being wrong rather than for being right soon enough. If you want to know which one you're running, look for the telltales, decisions that read well, dashboards that never spook you, and a roadmap that always fits the calendar.

The Bill You Don't See

It never arrives as an invoice. It shows up as drift. A quarter slips, a roadmap shrinks, a hire you needed joins someone else. Finance can't book it because nothing "happened." But caution accrues interest, and the compounding is quiet. By the ` balance is contact with reality at a cadence fast enough to learn, shipping while it still hurts, simplifying while it's still slower, deleting controls as aggressively as you added them. Until then, the bill remains invisible, perfectly rational, and right on time.

Conclusion: Safety as Strategy, Stasis as Outcome

Risk aversion doesn't kick down the door; it tidies the room. It speaks the language of stewardship, installs elegant guardrails, and delivers quarters that read well. But the compound effect is unmistakable: decision latency outruns build time, variance collapses into narratable safety, pilots outnumber products, launches huddle near optics windows, and the architecture fills with shims instead of spine. The dashboards turn green while the slope goes flat. What begins as "prudence" becomes a silent conversion of option value into paperwork, of learning loops into status reports, of ambition into alignment. You don't fall behind in a moment, you drift there, invoice by invisible invoice.

This is the hidden arithmetic of fear: every avoided bruise accrues as an unpaid balance, lost timing, constrained contracts, dulled teams, cautious customers, slower capital, thicker process. The ledger never arrives as a single line item; it shows up as a valuation that prices maintenance instead of momentum, a roadmap that always fits the calendar, a culture that can explain everything and change very little. Avoiding failure produces a different kind of failure, the slow, durable kind that feels responsible right up until it is irreversible.

So where do we go from here? We've mapped the mechanics: how caution seeps in, how it feels rational, how to measure it, and what it secretly costs. Now we pivot from diagnosis to design.

Part 3
Breaking the Cycle, Can Big Companies Innovate?

Every business story has a hauntingly familiar rhythm. A small, restless startup rewrites the rules. Its founders live close to the customer, close to the problem, close to the edge. The company grows, scales, dominates, and then, slowly, the tempo changes. Meetings multiply. Risk tolerance drops. What began as revolution becomes routine.

The disruptor becomes the incumbent. And the cycle begins again.

We've seen this movie too many times: Kodak invents digital photography and dies protecting film. Nokia builds the world's most loved phone and loses it to a touchscreen. Xerox, Blockbuster, BlackBerry, each one brilliant, each one confident, each one blindsided. Not because they lacked talent or money, but because success made them careful.

Even today's titans aren't immune. The bigger they get, the more gravity they generate, and gravity pulls everything toward safety. A company that once bet the future on unproven ideas now struggles to approve a color change in the logo. The tempo of invention slows to the tempo of the quarter.

But decline isn't destiny. Some companies break the cycle. Microsoft rebuilt its soul around curiosity after a decade of complacency. Amazon institutionalized reinvention, willing to obsolete its own products before anyone else could. Tesla operates at global scale but still moves like a startup, iterating in public, learning in real time, breaking things on purpose.

The myth of being *too big to innovate* is exactly that, a myth. What matters is not size, but system. Innovation doesn't die because you grew; it dies because you built the wrong habits for that size. The question isn't "Can big companies innovate?" The real question is: Can they design themselves to never stop?

This part of the book is about building those designs, the operating systems that let scale and imagination coexist. We'll explore what it takes to keep curiosity alive inside complexity:

- **Organizational agility** how to build flexible systems that bend without breaking.
- **Long-term bets vs. short-term pressure** how to protect the future without betraying the present.
- **AI and automation as amplifiers of creativity** how new tools can collapse time and expand insight.
- **Cultural rewiring** how to replace bureaucracy with rhythm, caution with speed, silence with signal.
- **Case studies that prove it's possible** stories of companies that refused to fossilize and rewrote their own maturity curve.

This is not a survival manual; it's a playbook for motion. Because the companies that thrive in the next decade won't be the biggest, they'll be the ones that learn the fastest. The ones that build curiosity into their code. The ones that treat "too big to innovate" as an insult, not an inevitability.

We live in an age where advantage decays faster than ever. AI is collapsing product cycles from years to months. Automation is redrawing how value is created. Global challengers emerge overnight with the velocity of startups and the ambition of empires. The incumbents that hesitate will be erased, not overtaken.

The companies that survive, the ones that lead, will be those that refuse to wait for the next disruption. They'll build it.

The cycle isn't fate. It's a choice. Let's explore how to break it, and how to stay broken, on purpose.

CHAPTER 7

Rebuilding an Innovation Culture

The Company That Forgot How to Breathe

Innovation doesn't die, it drifts. The lights stay on, the dashboards stay green, the meetings stay full. But the hum changes. The sound that once came from discovery now comes from maintenance. The work still moves, but not forward, just around.

No one chooses this. No leader wakes up and says, *let's make things slower.* It happens one safeguard at a time, one extra sign-off, one phrase like *"we'll revisit next quarter."* Slowly, the company that once pulsed with invention starts running on conservation. It doesn't collapse; it calcifies.

But decline is not destiny. The same system that taught caution can be taught movement again, if leaders learn to rewrite the rules of oxygen. Reversing the drift isn't a motivational exercise; it's a redesign of metabolism.

The first breath back is curiosity. Every revival begins when a team somewhere stops waiting for permission and starts asking better questions. What if the approval we fear isn't actually required? What if the customer already forgave the risk we're still managing? Renewal always starts below the waterline, in a single pocket of air, a product team that prototypes without a meeting, a manager who trades explanation for execution, a leader who asks, *"What would this look like if we were small again?"*

The second breath is speed. Not recklessness, but responsiveness, the ability to turn intent into motion without bureaucratic drag. Companies relearn speed by collapsing distance: decisions made where information lives, not three floors above it. Every unnecessary gate removed is a lung re-opened.

The third breath is learning. Innovation revives when error becomes education instead of evidence of failure. The moment teams see that an experiment gone wrong leads to promotion, not probation, the air changes. People stop protecting themselves and start improving the system.

When a company remembers these three breaths, curiosity, speed, learning, it remembers how to live in the future again. Meetings feel lighter. The hum returns. The metrics stop mattering more than the momentum.

Revival does not require tearing down the building; it requires reopening the vents. Remove one layer of defensive process. Shorten one feedback loop. Give one team the power to decide. Innovation returns the way spring does: quietly at first, then all at once.

What follows in this chapter is not theory, but a set of architectural interventions, ways to rebuild a system that conducts energy instead of storing it. Because innovation was never lost; it was just held under the weight of good intentions. And it only takes a few brave adjustments to let the company breathe again.

Remove Bureaucracy, Keep the Bones

Structure is not the enemy; friction without benefit is. The goal isn't chaos. It's *conductive structure*, an operating system that carries energy instead of absorbing it.

Every company that grows must choose its physics. In the early days, gravity is light, decisions fall quickly from thought to action. But as the organization scales, layers form to catch mistakes before they hit the ground. Those layers accumulate, and soon the same safety nets that once saved the company begin to trap its movement.

To rebuild innovation, a company must perform organizational surgery with a steady hand: cutting friction, not bone; removing fear, not discipline. The challenge is not to become *flat*, but to become *fluid*. Hierarchy is not evil, it's insulation. The question is how thick you let it get before it starts blocking the current.

Reversing bureaucracy begins with re-routing authority. In a healthy system, decisions live close to the data, not far from it. The people who build, test, and ship should also decide. Every approval you move upward loses a degree of truth. The air at the top may be clear, but it's thin, too far from the customer, too slow to breathe.

In practice, this means turning the pyramid into a network. Let leaders define principles, not permissions. Give teams their own oxygen supply: budgets they control, thresholds they can act within, boundaries they can bend when the situation demands. Empowerment is not a speech; it's a design choice.

Then, replace gates with guardrails. Gates assume distrust; guardrails assume intent. Instead of blocking motion until ten signatures appear, define the conditions under which motion is safe. A company that trusts its people enough to move learns faster than one that trusts its process to decide.

And finally, confront the hidden enemy of all momentum: meetings. Most meetings exist to prove alignment that systems should ensure automatically. When technology and transparency do their jobs, conversation becomes creation again, not a ritual of reassurance.

What emerges after this pruning is not anarchy, but clarity. Teams know what they can decide, what they must consult, and what only leadership can overrule. The chain of command stops being a chain and becomes a current.

The purpose of structure is to enable motion. When structure absorbs energy, it becomes bureaucracy. When it transmits energy, it becomes culture. The work of renewal lies in that distinction.

The next sections explore how to operationalize this shift: how to move decision-making to the edge, replace gates with guardrails, and rebuild the rhythms of speed without losing the strength of discipline.

1) Move Decisions to the Edge

Bureaucracy's favorite word is *alignment.* It sounds noble, collaborative, even. But alignment, when overdone, becomes delay wearing a polite name. The moment every decision must climb a ladder to be blessed, speed becomes theater, and innovation becomes a memory of how the company used to feel.

The truth is simple: information decays with distance. Every step a decision travels upward loses fidelity; every step it travels downward loses urgency. By the time an idea reaches the room where it can be approved, it no longer resembles the problem it was meant to solve.

Companies that rediscover innovation flip that logic, they move decisions to the edge, where knowledge is fresh and ownership is personal. They replace command-and-control with *trust-and-verify.* They don't flatten the hierarchy; they make it porous.

This shift is not a gesture of faith in people; it's an act of precision. The closer a decision lives to the facts, the better it fits reality. Teams on the ground know the constraints, the context, the customer's hesitation, the line of code that breaks, the vendor that's slow to ship. Yet in most large companies, those same teams must ask permission from people who only see the summary, not the story.

Leaders who move authority to the edge understand that speed is not recklessness, it's responsiveness. The goal isn't to eliminate control but to *relocate* it. Instead of senior executives approving the many, they approve the framework for the few:

- What kinds of bets are reversible, and therefore safe to make fast?
- What kinds of bets are one-way doors, and therefore deserve debate?
- What are the boundaries within which teams can decide and act without escalation?

These companies design decision bandwidth like engineers design circuits, wide enough to carry current, narrow enough to stay stable. They define *decision rights* by proximity to knowledge, not by job title.

At Amazon, this principle is encoded in the "two-pizza team", not a cute metaphor, but an operational philosophy. A team small enough to share a meal is small enough to make a call. Those teams decide quickly because they can see the entire consequence of their choice. The pizza isn't the point; the closed loop of accountability is.

Spotify applies the same logic differently. Its "squads" own a single feature end-to-end: design, build, deploy, measure. No committees, no dependencies, no long chain of signatures. The company doesn't trust speed to magic; it trusts it to ownership.

In both cases, the pattern is identical: proximity replaces permission.

When companies move decisions to the edge, two transformations occur. First, leaders stop being bottlenecks and start being context providers. Their job shifts from signing to shaping, defining purpose, constraints, and metrics of learning. Second, teams rediscover the feeling of movement. They stop optimizing presentations and start optimizing impact.

You know a company has reached this turning point when people no longer ask, *"Who needs to sign off?"* but *"Who needs to know?"* That subtle change in language marks the return of trust, and with it, speed.

The next step is to protect that trust from suffocation. Because freedom without structure burns out as fast as control kills it. The balance lies in design, replacing gates with guardrails, so the organization can move quickly without falling apart.

2) Replace Gates with Guardrails

Every bureaucracy begins with a good reason. Someone once made a mistake, and a rule was born to prevent its twin. Over time, those rules multiply faster than the problems they were meant to solve. Each new safeguard promises protection. Together, they deliver paralysis.

When every project must pass through ten gates to prove it won't fail, failure simply moves upstream. It doesn't disappear, it waits. The company feels safer but becomes slower, its creativity checked not by catastrophe but by compliance.

Innovation suffocates in that kind of safety. You can't prototype your way to the future if you need a signature for every step. But removing gates entirely is no solution either. Chaos moves quickly, but it rarely arrives anywhere worth going. The art lies in *guardrails*: enough structure to prevent disaster, but not enough to prevent discovery.

A gate says, *stop until you're approved*. A guardrail says, *move fast, just stay on the road*.

The best organizations design for motion, not permission. They codify principles instead of approvals. They replace lengthy checklists with living frameworks that tell teams how to think, not what to think.

Netflix's famous "freedom and responsibility" culture document isn't a manifesto; it's an operating manual for guardrails. Employees are trusted to make expensive decisions because the system assumes judgment, not obedience. Amazon does the same with its "one-way vs. two-way door" framework: reversible decisions are made fast and locally; irreversible ones earn deliberation. Both systems treat speed as a form of respect, for the idea, for the customer, for the moment.

Guardrails thrive on transparency, not control. Instead of reviews behind closed doors, information flows in daylight. Dashboards update in real time. Teams share metrics, learnings, and reversals openly, not as performances but as part of the collective brain. The result is a culture where oversight happens continuously, not episodically. No need for ten signatures when visibility is built into the work.

The real test of guardrails is emotional, not procedural. It's whether leaders can watch a team make a small mistake and resist the instinct to build a new rule. Most organizations don't lack process, they lack tolerance. Guardrails demand the opposite of bureaucracy's reflex: instead of tightening after every bump, you learn from the curve.

In a guardrail culture, error becomes signal. When something breaks, the question isn't *who approved this?* but *what did this teach us?* The post-mortem becomes a design document for better systems, not a trial for blame. That's how a company develops agility that lasts longer than the next reorg.

This kind of structure doesn't make the company reckless, it makes it *alive*. Ideas move through fewer checkpoints and more experiments. Teams launch sooner, learn faster, and recover smarter. The organization stops fearing motion and starts metabolizing it.

Guardrails let the company breathe without hyperventilating. They turn governance into guidance, control into context, and oversight into learning. They give permission back to the people who can use it best.

When you see them working, you can feel it. Meetings shorten. Feedback loops tighten. The distance between idea and action collapses. What once took a quarter takes a week, not because anyone skipped steps, but because the steps stopped tripping over each other.

The next challenge is sustaining that rhythm at scale, ensuring that speed doesn't burn itself out, that energy doesn't scatter faster than it compounds. That's where technology and design come in. The next section explores how modern systems, data, automation, and AI, can replace bureaucracy's manual brakes with intelligence that keeps the company fast *and* safe.

3) Kill Meeting Debt

Every company accumulates debt. Financial debt you can measure; technical debt you can refactor. But meeting debt, wasted hours disguised as alignment, just compounds quietly until curiosity goes bankrupt.

The larger the organization, the more it worships the calendar. When motion stalls, someone schedules a meeting. When progress is unclear, someone schedules two. Soon, days become a grid of apologies for real work deferred.

Meetings begin as instruments of coordination and end as proof of existence. We meet to report, to update, to "sync." But nothing syncs, information is repeated, not advanced. Everyone leaves informed but unchanged. The work moves again only once the meeting ends.

This is meeting debt: the time tax of a system that doesn't trust itself to think asynchronously.

The cure isn't the fantasy of a "meeting-free culture." Coordination is essential; collaboration is oxygen. The problem isn't the meeting, it's what meetings have become: a crutch for unclear ownership, lazy communication, and manual oversight that better systems should already provide.

Killing meeting debt starts with a structural audit, not a calendar cleanse. For every recurring meeting, ask:

- What decision dies if this meeting disappears?

- What question could a shared dashboard or written memo answer faster?
- Who's here because they must decide versus because they might be blamed later?

If no one can name the decision, delete the invite. You haven't canceled collaboration, you've reclaimed attention.

The most innovative organizations treat meetings as high-cost instruments, reserved for *thinking together*, not *reporting apart*. Amazon institutionalized this discipline with the six-page narrative memo. Before every meeting, participants read silently, no slides, no performance, no multitasking. The document becomes a mirror: if the idea isn't clear in writing, it isn't ready for discussion. Meetings shrink in number and expand in quality.

Asynchronous systems finish the job. Shared workspaces, AI-generated summaries, and automated updates make status meetings obsolete. Transparency replaces talk. When information flows freely, meetings regain their original purpose: to make decisions that require human friction, debate, intuition, tradeoffs, judgment.

But killing meeting debt is ultimately a cultural act. It means teaching that absence from the room is not absence from the mission. That reading is participation. That silence doesn't mean disengagement; it means trust that others will carry the conversation forward.

The payoff is immediate. Calendars open. Thought returns. Teams rediscover deep work, the kind that produces breakthroughs, not slide decks. Managers rediscover leadership as foresight, not facilitation. The company starts measuring its productivity not by hours spoken but by ideas shipped.

When meeting debt dies, energy returns. The corridors quiet, but the work hums. Oversight has become ambient, alignment automatic, and collaboration intentional. People meet when it matters. The rest of the time, they build.

That is the first signal a company is breathing again.

4) Automate the Oversight

Bureaucracy grows wherever trust decays. Each report, each sign-off, each meeting to "ensure visibility" is a substitute for confidence that the work is being done well. Oversight, in its healthiest form, is guidance; in its bureaucratic form, it's surveillance.

The cure isn't less oversight, it's *smarter* oversight. When information can flow continuously, you don't need a meeting to confirm reality. When the system knows where things stand, leaders can spend their time shaping direction instead of auditing execution.

The paradox of large organizations is that they often collect oceans of data yet see only puddles of truth. Status lives in spreadsheets, updates in email threads, metrics in disconnected dashboards. Every tool exists to inform, but none to integrate. The result is noise disguised as diligence.

Automating oversight begins by wiring the system to watch itself. Not with more dashboards, but with connective tissue, data that moves automatically to where it's needed, in real time, without human relays.

AI-driven tools can now do what committees once pretended to:

- Detect anomalies before they become crises.
- Track dependencies across teams and flag when one delay will cascade.

- Compare forecast to reality continuously, not quarterly.
- Verify compliance silently, in the background, instead of through rituals of self-reporting.

When this automation works, the company stops managing through meetings. Oversight becomes *ambient*, always on, always visible, always updating. Problems surface themselves; accountability becomes self-evident. Teams don't need to prepare slides about performance; they improve performance.

Leaders, freed from the administrative fog, regain their real job: interpretation and intervention. They stop asking, "Where are we?" and start asking, "What did we learn?" The review becomes a conversation about decisions, not documentation.

Automated oversight also dissolves one of bureaucracy's most subtle toxins: selective visibility. When information flows naturally, no one can hide behind partial truths or favorable framing. Transparency stops being a performance and starts being an architecture.

But automation alone isn't liberation. A company can drown in real-time metrics just as easily as it suffocated under quarterly decks. The point isn't to watch everything; it's to design systems that watch the *right* things. Oversight should amplify awareness, not anxiety.

The best systems are invisible: present everywhere, discussed nowhere. They make accountability an atmosphere rather than an event. They allow leaders to lead by principle, not by proximity.

When oversight becomes effortless, permission expands. People move faster because they know the guardrails are real. Risk becomes calculable again. And with that, innovation, once trapped in process, starts breathing on its own.

The next step is to protect that oxygen. Automation can expose reality, but only culture can act on it. The real work is rebuilding the reflex to move, rekindling curiosity, rediscovering ownership, and making bold decisions feel less like defiance and more like duty.

5) Make Risk Safe

Once the systems are clean and the air starts moving again, the question becomes human: Will anyone dare to breathe deeply?

You can dismantle bureaucracy, automate oversight, and kill the meeting debt that suffocated your calendar, but none of it matters if people are still afraid. Fear doesn't need process to survive; it only needs memory. It lingers in the small calculations every employee makes before raising a hand, in the quiet edit of an idea before it's spoken, in the habit of asking permission for things that used to be instinct.

The problem isn't that people hate risk. They hate *being punished for it.*

To rebuild innovation, a company must make risk safe, not by eliminating consequences, but by reframing them. The goal is not recklessness; it's recoverability. Innovation is not the art of being right, it's the discipline of being wrong safely, and learning faster than your competitors.

Great organizations institutionalize that safety. They don't tell people to "be bold"; they build systems that absorb the shock of boldness.

- **Small bets, reversible moves.** Create sandboxes where experiments can fail without infecting the core.

- **Rapid feedback loops.** Replace postmortems with *premortems*, discussions about what could go wrong before it does, so learning starts early.
- **Public debriefs, not private blame.** Normalize transparency around missteps; treat them as shared data, not personal shame.

When risk becomes part of the rhythm, courage stops being heroic, it becomes routine.

One of the most common corporate myths is that innovation requires visionary leaders who defy rules. In truth, it requires systems that make rule-breaking unnecessary. When you design for reversible decisions and fast recovery, you give everyone permission to act without fear of permanent damage. Amazon calls these "two-way doors": decisions you can walk through and back again. The result isn't chaos, it's circulation.

But safety isn't built by policy alone. It's taught by observation. Employees learn what risk means not from handbooks, but from how leaders react when things go wrong. A single punishment for a failed experiment can erase a year of cultural reform. Conversely, a single public thank-you for a thoughtful failure can reset the tone for an entire company.

Making risk safe also means widening the definition of success. If every metric rewards short-term certainty, no one will bet on long-term ambiguity. That's why innovation cultures need parallel currencies, recognition for learning velocity, for experiments run, for insights gained even when outcomes fail. Progress becomes multidimensional: not just revenue, but readiness.

Over time, safety produces speed. The company stops waiting for proof before it moves. It acts, measures, adapts. Fear becomes friction, not paralysis. Leaders spend less time granting permission and more time expanding the radius of trust.

When risk becomes safe, curiosity returns. People start asking "what if" again. The company regains its appetite for the unknown.

Because innovation isn't born from fearlessness, it's born from systems that make fear survivable.

And once an organization learns to live with that kind of risk, it stops managing the future and starts *making* it.

6) Rebuild the Rhythm

Speed alone isn't strength. Many companies rediscover motion only to lose direction, ideas flying faster than the system can absorb, energy without coherence, velocity without rhythm. Innovation doesn't need chaos; it needs cadence.

Rebuilding the rhythm is about restoring *pulse*, the steady alternation between exploration and execution, freedom and focus, movement and meaning. It's how a company learns to breathe again, not in gasps but in cycles.

The first step is temporal honesty, acknowledging that not all work moves on the same clock. Discovery beats to curiosity's tempo; delivery beats to discipline's. When you force both onto the same calendar, you smother one and exhaust the other. Healthy organizations learn to sync these rhythms without making them identical. They let exploration wander while ensuring execution lands.

That means designing rituals that reinforce tempo instead of replacing it.

- Replace the annual plan with a living roadmap, a strategy that updates as the world does.
- Replace quarterly reviews with rolling narratives that tell not just *what happened*, but *what changed because of it*.
- Replace static KPIs with dynamic signals, leading indicators of learning, not just lagging indicators of success.

In this rhythm, feedback becomes music, not noise. Each loop, experiment, reflection, iteration, adds a note to the company's memory. The organization develops a kind of muscle memory for adaptation. You don't need to remind people to innovate; they just do, because the tempo carries them.

Leadership sets this rhythm by how it measures progress. The companies that sustain innovation measure tempo, not theatre. They care less about how many projects launch and more about how quickly insight turns into action. They treat speed as a cultural asset, not a quarterly accident.

But rhythm isn't just operational, it's emotional. It's the feeling that the work has a pulse again. That decisions arrive when the moment still matters. That people can see how their effort joins a larger movement. When that alignment clicks, you can feel it in the hallways: fewer updates, more breakthroughs; fewer "check-ins," more *checkpoints*. The air feels lighter because time has meaning again.

Rebuilding rhythm also means accepting rest. Burnout is just bureaucracy's evil twin, different costume, same paralysis. A company that runs at full sprint without pause doesn't innovate; it erodes. The rhythm must include recovery, spaces for thinking, for curiosity, for reflection unmeasured by output. In those pauses, insight accumulates.

The real signal that rhythm has returned isn't speed, it's sync. Teams stop tripping over one another. Data flows without translation. Decisions land while they're still relevant. The company starts to feel less like an organization and more like an organism, coordinated, alert, alive.

When that happens, innovation stops being a project and becomes a reflex. Bureaucracy no longer absorbs motion; it channels it. Leadership no longer demands urgency; it sustains it.

A company that has rebuilt its rhythm no longer fears time. It uses it.

And that is when it truly begins to lead again.

Build Places Where the Future Can Start

You don't need a separate building to do bold work. But you do need separate rules.

Innovation rarely dies from lack of ideas; it dies from exposure. A fragile concept, born in a system optimized for predictability, doesn't get oxygen long enough to prove itself. That's why even the most forward-looking companies need protected habitats, spaces where uncertainty isn't punished, and the future can take its first breath without being audited for ROI on day one.

The goal isn't isolation. It's insulation, just enough distance for ideas to grow, without losing the connection that makes them valuable.

The Skunkworks, Reimagined

Independent enough to move. Connected enough to matter.

The classic Skunkworks model, born in secrecy, fueled by urgency, has been mythologized as innovation's purest form. But in practice, too many corporate versions become museums of demos: beautiful prototypes that never found a home. They were protected so well that they forgot why they existed.

The modern Skunkworks needs a different charter. It doesn't hide from the company; it teaches it. Its purpose is not rebellion, it's renewal.

Charter:

Three to five bets a year that would break a current rule to unlock a future line of business. Not research for its own sake, but intentional heresy: projects that test what the company forbids, neglects, or fears to attempt.

Funding:

A multi-year pool, ring-fenced from quarterly raids. Innovation cannot sprint to the rhythm of the P&L; it must run on conviction, not convenience. Protect the capital, or you will end up funding slides instead of science.

Interfaces:

Clarity is oxygen. The Skunkworks should have exactly three lines of connection:

- One executive sponsor with real budget authority, not ceremonial endorsement.

- One *intake door* for ideas and needs that the core cannot yet handle.
- One *on-ramp back*, the explicit pathway for integration once an experiment proves itself.

Everything else, branding, office space, secrecy, is theater unless these interfaces work.

Exit Criteria: Every project must answer two questions from the start:

1. If it works, who owns it, when, and under what metric does it shift from "experimental" to "P&L"?
2. If it fails, how do we recycle the code, the talent, and the learning within 30 days?

Failure without recycling is waste. Success without ownership is drift.

Wrong Skunkworks: A museum of demos, brilliant artifacts behind glass, visited occasionally by executives who nod and leave unchanged.

Right Skunkworks: A factory that ships back standards the core can adopt, technologies, methods, and cultural upgrades that raise the baseline for everyone else.

When done right, the Skunkworks doesn't escape the company; it expands it. It gives the organization a second metabolism, a faster, hungrier one, that metabolizes uncertainty before the market does.

Because the future doesn't need a new building. It needs a place inside the old one where tomorrow is allowed to start.

Case Study: The Skunkworks That Saved a Company , Lockheed, 1943

Every era rediscovers the need for a Skunkworks. The name comes from the first one, born not from theory, but from panic.

In 1943, Lockheed was weeks behind a rival on a wartime jet-fighter contract. The Air Force wanted a prototype in 180 days, an impossible timeline inside the company's own machinery. The bureaucracy that protected precision had become a liability. So they did something radical: they stepped outside of it.

Kelly Johnson, a 33-year-old engineer, took 23 people, commandeered a rented circus tent near a foul-smelling plastics plant, and told his team they would build the future on their own clock. No committees. No memos. One page of rules.

He called it the Skunk Works, half-joke, half-provocation.

The result: the XP-80 Shooting Star, the first operational U.S. jet fighter, delivered in 143 days, 37 days ahead of the impossible schedule.

Johnson's genius wasn't just engineering; it was operating design. He stripped out the layers that slowed decisions, flattened hierarchies, and made the work self-governing. His 14 "rules" became the foundation of modern innovation doctrine:

- Small, elite teams.
- Direct communication with the customer.
- Minimal reporting.
- Empowered engineers who could sign for their own parts.
- "A good idea today is better than a perfect idea next week."

The Skunk Works didn't just build planes, it built a culture where trust replaced process. Over the next five decades, it produced the U-2, the SR-71 Blackbird, and the F-117 Nighthawk, each one redefining what was possible in aerospace.

The lesson wasn't speed for its own sake. It was structural clarity: the recognition that creativity suffocates under divided authority. Every breakthrough followed the same pattern, autonomy at the edge, accountability at the core.

Modern companies still chase this blueprint, but most only copy the aesthetic (secret rooms, black budgets, slick branding) without the discipline. They forget that the original Skunk Works was not a rebel camp; it was a contract of trust, leaders willing to surrender control in exchange for results.

That is the real power of the model:

- Freedom with consequences.
- Speed with responsibility.
- Chaos contained by purpose.

The companies that remember those ingredients can still do in months what others do in years.

Because the Skunk Works wasn't about secrecy. It was about permission, the permission to move at the speed of necessity.

Case Study: Lab126, Shipping the Future Back to the Mothership (Amazon, 2004–)

Amazon didn't build a separate building for bold work; it built separate rules and put them in a unit called Lab126. The brief was heretical at the time: a retailer would design hardware. The charter was simple and sharp, make reading digital feel inevitable, and later, turn the home into a voice interface.

What worked wasn't secrecy; it was operating design:

- **Small, sovereign teams** with authority over roadmap, industrial design, and go-to-market.
- **Ring-fenced, multi-year funding** insulated from the retail P&L's weekly gravity.
- **A single, empowered interface** back to the core (Bezos as sponsor; later a tight exec loop) so decisions didn't drown in committees.
- **Explicit exits**: if a device proved pull (engagement, retention, attach), it graduated into the Amazon flywheel, content, Prime, commerce, Alexa skills.

Kindle didn't just ship a device; it standardized a pipeline, content ingestion, Whispernet, DRM, pricing, that the core business could adopt. Echo didn't just add a speaker; it taught the company how to build and maintain a living platform (wake words, skills, far-field updates) and pushed Amazon into ambient computing. Wins were absorbed; methods became standards.

The lesson is Skunkworks-by-integration: independent enough to move; connected enough to matter. Lab126 wasn't a museum of demos; it was a factory that shipped back capabilities the core could scale.

Case Study: X, Betting on the Underspecified Future (Alphabet, 2010–)

Alphabet's X (the "Moonshot Factory") is Skunkworks for problems that don't fit quarterly logic. The unit exists to break a current rule (unit economics, physics, or industry boundary) and either prove it or kill it cleanly.

Its operating code mirrors the original Skunk Works, updated for software and services:

- **Charter:** Tackle N=1 problems with N-of-many impact (mobility, comms, climate).
- **Funding:** Multi-year, insulated capital; kill projects early without stigma (e.g., **Loon** sunset with a public technical postmortem; IP and know-how recycled).
- **Interfaces:** One exec sponsor; one intake from Google/Alphabet; one defined on-ramp back (spin-out, spin-in, or wind-down).
- **Exit criteria:** If it works, it becomes a company (Waymo, Wing, Verily) or a core platform contribution; if not, the learning is documented and redistributed.

Crucially, X optimizes for truth per dollar, not optics per quarter. That's why it can both graduate (Waymo's autonomy stack) and gracefully retire (Makani, Loon) without poisoning culture. In both cases, the organization gains: capabilities, standards, scar tissue, institutional memory that compounds.

What These Skunkworks Share

- A narrow, heretical charter (do what the core currently forbids).
- Sovereign time and money (multi-year, ring-fenced).
- Simple, enforced interfaces (one sponsor, one intake, one on-ramp back).
- Explicit exits (graduate to P&L with owning team and metrics, or recycle code/talent/learning in 30 days).

And the non-negotiable:

- They ship standards back to the core. Tools, pipelines, governance patterns, the reusable scaffolding that raises everyone's ceiling.

That's the difference between a demo museum and a future factory. The former entertains; the latter changes the company's default.

Intrapreneurs at Scale (Without Turning Everyone Into a Founder)

The most underused asset in a big company isn't capital or data, it's the people who still see like it's day one but have learned where the bodies are buried. They understand both the machine and its ghosts. They know how things break and how to fix them, if only someone would let them try.

Scaling intrapreneurship isn't about making everyone a founder. It's about designing a system where the few who still burn with that early light can act without begging for permission. Structure doesn't kill creativity, lack of agency does.

1) Create a Standing Seed Fund

Every large company claims it wants "more ideas," but ideas without oxygen just decorate slide decks. What intrapreneurs need is not applause but capital, small, fast, renewable bets that let them prove signal before the antibodies arrive.

The mechanics:

- **Ticket size:** $10k–$250k for 60–90 day proofs. Small enough to move quietly, big enough to get real data.

- **Gate:** One page, one metric, one customer. No ten-slide decks, no venture-theater. The point is to reduce permission to its essence: show a hypothesis worth testing and a metric worth watching.
- **Ownership:** If the month proves signal, the project graduates, to a real owner with time, budget, and a roadmap. If it doesn't, it dies cleanly, with a short write-up archived in a searchable library of "smart failures."

The goal isn't volume; it's velocity of learning. A company that can run a hundred $25,000 tests faster than one $2.5M program learns at startup speed again.

2) Make Failure Economical and Public

Fear of failure is the invisible tax on innovation. It's not the cost of mistakes that hurts companies, it's the silence that follows them. When teams hide what they learned because they fear career risk, the organization pays twice: once for the loss, and again for the secrecy.

The countermeasure: build ritual around transparency.

- **Hall of Tries:** A monthly 20-minute session where one team presents what didn't work and what they learned. No postmortem theatre, no blame, just evidence and curiosity.
- **Career safety:** Write it down in policy, not folklore. A failed, well-run test should count positively in performance reviews. Reward the discipline of learning over the illusion of perfection.

Public failure normalizes curiosity. It tells the company: we don't punish hypotheses; we punish silence.

3) Cross-Functional by Default

Innovation dies fastest at the borders. The moment an idea has to "handoff," it starts to lose heat.

The fix isn't alignment meetings, it's structural from day one. If the problem crosses org lines, the team must too.

The model:

- **Trios:** Product + Engineering + Ops/Go-to-Market assigned from the start. One team, three lenses, zero translation loss.
- **Shared scoreboard:** A single metric that everyone can see, own, and move, customer conversion, retention lift, time-to-value. The number doesn't care about swim lanes; neither should the team.

Cross-functionality isn't decoration; it's insulation against entropy. It keeps the learning loop closed and the language coherent.

4) A Path Out of the Sandbox

Most corporate "innovation" dies in the petting zoo, endless pilots, eternal demos, proofs of concept that never touch a customer at scale. The tragedy isn't that they fail; it's that they succeed quietly and are never allowed to grow.

The discipline:

- **Ramp plan:** Define pre-agreed thresholds (X retention, Y gross margin, Z risk posture) that automatically trigger funding, staffing, and a home inside the core business.
- **Kill equal to scale:** The same thresholds that promote a win should terminate a near-miss. No zombies. If it didn't clear the bar, shut it down, document it, and recycle what's useful.

Scaling innovation requires symmetry. Reward as publicly as you retire. Celebrate the clarity that ends a project as much as the one that graduates.

The Operating Model That Keeps You Honest

A company can rediscover speed, rebuild rhythm, even light up pockets of invention, but if the system doesn't *stay honest*, entropy returns. Innovation decays not because people forget how to dream, but because the operating model quietly forgets how to measure what matters.

This is the antidote: a structure that keeps invention accountable without turning it back into bureaucracy. A system that keeps the corridors clear, the clocks aligned, and the language coherent.

Own the Seam

The corridor between functions is where ambition goes to stall. It's nobody's budget, nobody's KPI, nobody's job to fix. So it fills with drift, handoffs that take weeks, definitions that diverge, and projects that "almost shipped."

Owning the seam means giving that in-between space a name, a leader, and a ledger.

Design it like this:

- **Seam metrics on page one:** Time to *true activation* (idea to customer use). Percentage of changes requiring three or more approvals. Fork count in core systems. Days from customer signal → shipped change. These are the numbers that reveal if the company is actually moving or just talking about moving.

- **Right to trade local green for global gain.** Every cross-functional leader must have explicit authority to turn off a "green" local metric (e.g., a team's perfect uptime or margin) if doing so accelerates a global outcome (faster learning, better experience, unified platform).

Without this power, collaboration becomes performance art, a ritual of consensus that costs velocity and yields nothing new. True ownership of the seam turns politeness into progress.

Two Clocks, One Plan

Every company runs on two rhythms: the rhythm of discovery and the rhythm of delivery. Innovation beats in learning cycles; the business beats in quarters. When you pretend they're the same clock, one will suffocate the other.

The rule: keep both visible and synchronized without forcing them to tick together.

- **Learning cadence:** Weekly: *What did we believe? What did we learn? What did we change?* Learning is an operating rhythm, not a special event. It should produce data as predictable as revenue, evidence that curiosity is still alive.
- **Quarterly bridge:** Once a quarter, translate what was learned into business terms, *impact on cost, margin, risk, or customer value*, without demanding that learning happen on the quarter's edge. This is where innovation earns its credibility.

If leadership doesn't protect both clocks, discovery gets resized to fit the quarter. That's when learning dies quietly, on time and out of meaning.

Two clocks, one plan: the company moves fast enough to learn and slow enough to last.

Language Without Drift

Words are operating systems. When they fork, truth follows.

Large companies rarely lose alignment through malice; they lose it through *semantic erosion*. "Activation" means one thing to Marketing, another to Product. "Reliability" looks green in one dashboard and red in another. Eventually, the company stops arguing about customers and starts negotiating definitions.

The countermeasure: institutionalize clarity.

- **Glossary with teeth:** Every core metric, activation, MAU, retention, reliability, must have a single owner: a cross-functional council empowered to redefine terms and update dashboards within a week.
- **Definition-to-dashboard pipeline:** When a word changes, the data follows, automatically. No PDF, no memo. The system rewires itself to reflect the new truth.

This sounds trivial until you realize how many decisions die from language drift. Innovation is execution at the speed of shared meaning. When words travel cleanly, action does too.

A company stays innovative not by chasing novelty, but by protecting honesty, between teams, between clocks, between words.

Own the seam. Align the clocks. Standardize the language.

That's how you keep a living system alive.

Field Guide, Ten Moves in Ten Weeks

You don't rebuild culture with memos. You rebuild it with momentum.

Innovation doesn't return because you said the right words in a town hall. It returns the moment people notice that decisions are moving faster, meetings are thinning out, and ideas are no longer dying in the hallway between "approved" and "in flight."

Every large company that finds its way back to speed begins the same way: a handful of deliberate, visible moves that tell the organization, *"we're serious this time."* Not symbolic gestures, structural edits that make curiosity safe and learning measurable.

You don't need a three-year transformation plan. You need ten bold acts in ten weeks, each one small enough to execute immediately, and big enough to change the emotional temperature of the company.

The pattern is simple:

- Fix who decides.
- Free who moves.
- Fund who tries.
- Celebrate who learns.
- Retire what no longer earns its oxygen.

Each of these moves does two things at once: it removes drag and signals permission. Taken together, they rewire the company's metabolism.

Here's the field guide. Ten weeks. Ten proof points that innovation isn't a speech, it's a system waking back up.

Field Guide, Ten Moves in Ten Weeks

1. **Publish decision rights for top 5 cross-org initiatives.** End the fog. Clarity is the cheapest accelerant.

2. **Slash approvals: three risk tiers, one page per tier.** Replace ritual with judgment. The cost of delay is a risk, too.

3. **Cut 30% of recurring meetings; replace with decision receipts.** Meetings don't move work; decisions do. Publish them. Let people see the system breathing again.

4. **Stand up a seam leader with budget and veto over local KPIs.** Someone must own the corridor between silos, or it owns you.

5. **Launch a seed fund; approve the first three $25k proofs this month.** Learning needs currency. Make small bets fast, and make the learning public.

6. **Adopt a default legal pack for common experiments.** Stop letting paperwork be the gatekeeper of curiosity.

7. **Make seam metrics page one of the staff deck.** If you don't measure the space between teams, you're not measuring speed, you're measuring theater.

8. **Create a 90-day skunkworks charter with one exec owner.** Independence isn't an indulgence; it's a pilot of what's possible when permission meets purpose.

9. **Add a Hall of Tries to your all-hands. Celebrate the best failed bet.** Make it public that failure is the tuition you pay for originality.

10. **Kill one zombie: reclaim its people, publish the learning.** A company that can't bury the dead can't birth the new.

Ten moves. Ten weeks.

Not transformation, proof of life.

After that, the organization will no longer ask *if* innovation is possible. It will know what it feels like when the company starts to move again.

What Changes When This Works

When the machinery of innovation starts working again, the change isn't just visible, it's audible. The tempo shifts, the language sharpens, the meetings shorten. You can tell a company is alive by the way it starts to decide again.

• **Tempo: Decisions happen where the facts live.** When decision rights finally sit with the people who hold the data, not the titles, the delay between insight and action collapses. Engineers stop waiting for executive reviews to fix what's obviously broken. Product teams stop presenting for permission and start shipping for proof. The calendar speeds up, not because anyone said, "go faster," but because the work stopped needing translation.

• **Truth: Post-mortems route to causes, not org charts.** In a healthy system, failure doesn't travel upward as a political story. It travels sideways as information. When post-mortems aim for truth instead of blame, the company gets smarter without getting meaner. Patterns emerge, not scapegoats. Every miss becomes a multiplier, a shared scar that raises collective judgment.

• **Talent: Builders stop interviewing elsewhere because the company started interviewing itself.** Great people don't leave for money; they leave for motion. When an organization starts asking itself the questions its best people were already asking, What's slowing us down? What's worth building next?, it reclaims its own curiosity. Builders stay because they can once again see their fingerprints on the future.

• **Cost: You spend less political capital and more code.** Energy stops bleeding into alignment meetings, defensive decks, and internal lobbying. The resources that once kept the machine polished now keep it moving. The company stops managing innovation and starts producing it , in code, in prototypes, in market signals.

This is not romance. It's mechanics.

Systems either conduct energy or they dampen it. When you rebuild the way work flows, who decides, who learns, who owns the seam, you change the company's basic physics.

Rebuilding an innovation culture is not about slogans or offsites. It's the deliberate act of **turning insulation into wire**, so that energy can move freely again, from insight to action, from curiosity to impact.

And when that current starts flowing, the company remembers what it was built to do: **not protect what it has, but build what comes next.**

Conclusion: Designing for Motion

Innovation isn't a department; it's an operating temperature. Every company runs on heat, the energy between idea and action, between conviction and proof. When that temperature drops, people stop arguing about what's possible and start debating what's permissible.

You don't raise it with slogans. You raise it with design.

Design is how culture becomes executable , decision rights at the edge, where the facts live; guardrails instead of gates, so judgment replaces permission; a funded corridor between teams, so collaboration isn't an afterthought; small bets with short half-lives, so learning compounds faster than politics; and a way for the future to come home, so experiments don't die in exile.

When those systems align, motion returns. The company remembers how to breathe, decisions flow, feedback loops shorten, and people rediscover the satisfaction of building something that didn't exist yesterday.

The irony is that innovation never really disappears; it just gets displaced by friction. The work of leadership is not to "inspire creativity," but to reduce the drag that makes it impossible. The systems that slow bad decisions also slow good ones. The goal isn't control, it's conductivity.

Get that right, and energy starts moving again. Curiosity becomes rhythm. Meetings turn into movement. The company stops rehearsing innovation and starts performing it.

Because motion, once restored, is self-sustaining. It attracts talent, generates truth, and keeps the organization young, not by age, but by metabolism.

CHAPTER 8

Balancing Growth and Disruption

For large corporations, one of the greatest challenges is balancing the need for sustainable growth with the imperative for disruption. While growth ensures stability, profitability, and investor confidence, disruption drives innovation, competitiveness, and long-term survival. The tension between these two forces is what often stalls innovation in large organizations: leaders are torn between protecting their existing revenue streams and making bold bets on the future.

At its core, the challenge of balancing growth and disruption arises from a fundamental paradox: successful companies become industry leaders by pioneering innovative products, services, and business models, yet as they scale, they prioritize efficiency, predictability, and risk management over the very experimentation that made them successful in the first place. This shift can cause companies to become victims of their own success: leading to stagnation, resistance to change, and an overreliance on legacy business models. The longer an organization delays its disruptive efforts, the more vulnerable it becomes to agile competitors, market shifts, and emerging technologies.

Consider some of the biggest corporate failures in history: Blockbuster, Kodak, Nokia, and Xerox, all of which were once dominant in their respective industries. Each of these companies had the resources, the expertise, and even the technological foresight to

214

disrupt their own markets, but their focus on short-term financial performance and protecting existing revenue streams prevented them from acting. By the time they acknowledged the shift in their industries, it was already too late.

On the other hand, companies like Amazon, Apple, and Tesla have managed to maintain steady growth while also fostering a culture of ongoing disruption. Amazon's e-commerce empire has expanded while simultaneously launching AWS, Alexa, and its cloud-based infrastructure. Apple has continued to evolve its product ecosystem, moving from computers to mobile devices, wearables, and digital services, ensuring it is never too dependent on a single product category. Tesla, despite early skepticism, has successfully scaled production while continuing to push forward with new energy solutions, automation, and AI-driven advancements in self-driving technology.

The key takeaway from these examples is that companies that master the balance between growth and disruption don't view them as opposing forces but as complementary elements of a successful long-term strategy. Instead of treating disruptive efforts as external threats to stability, they embed innovation within their organizational DNA, creating structures that support both sustained growth and continuous reinvention.

This chapter explores how businesses can navigate the delicate balance between growth and disruption, ensuring that they remain competitive without stagnating. By examining structural strategies, leadership approaches, and case studies, we will highlight how companies can foster controlled disruption while maintaining financial health. The goal is not to choose between growth and innovation, but to develop a corporate strategy that allows both to thrive simultaneously.

How Companies Can Resolve the Growth-Innovation Paradox

While the growth-innovation paradox presents a significant challenge, companies that actively acknowledge and address it can develop strategies to integrate disruption into their business models. The key is to build structures that allow innovation to thrive without compromising financial stability. Some of the most effective approaches include:

1. **Creating Separate Innovation Units**
   - By establishing Skunkworks teams or dedicated innovation labs, companies can allow disruptive ideas to develop without interference from the core business.
   - For example, Alphabet's X (Moonshot Factory) operates separately from Google's main business, allowing it to explore radical new technologies without the pressure of quarterly earnings reports.

2. **Developing a Portfolio Approach to Innovation**
   - Companies should balance incremental improvements in their core business with high-risk, high-reward investments in disruptive technologies.
   - Amazon, for example, continuously launches new ventures, some of which fail (like the Fire Phone), but others, such as AWS, become massive growth engines.

3. **Structuring Innovation Around Long-Term Goals**

- Leadership must align innovation efforts with long-term strategic priorities, rather than focusing solely on short-term financial performance.
- Tesla's investment in AI-driven self-driving capabilities, despite years of losses, demonstrates a commitment to long-term market leadership.

4. **Fostering a Culture of Experimentation**
   - Companies must build psychological safety, where employees feel comfortable taking risks without fear of career repercussions.
   - Google's 20%-time policy, which allowed employees to dedicate part of their workweek to personal projects, led to innovations like Gmail and Google Maps.

By integrating these strategies, companies can turn the growth-innovation paradox into a competitive advantage, leveraging their scale and resources to drive innovation, rather than allowing them to become barriers to progress.

In the following sections, we will explore how business leaders can implement these principles in practice, using real-world case studies of companies that have successfully maintained growth while embracing disruption.

Building an Innovation Ecosystem Within a Growing Business

For companies to achieve both sustained growth and continued innovation, they must go beyond isolated R&D efforts and create a structured innovation ecosystem: one that allows new ideas to be explored, tested, and integrated into the broader organization without disrupting core operations.

A strong innovation ecosystem operates on multiple levels, combining internal experimentation, external partnerships, and a fluid structure that enables the company to evolve while continuing to scale. The following strategies illustrate how companies can build and sustain this type of ecosystem without hindering financial performance.

1. Defining a Strategic Innovation Framework

Many companies struggle with innovation not because they lack ideas, but because they lack a strategic framework for prioritizing and integrating those ideas into the business. An innovation ecosystem should be structured around three key categories:

- **Core Innovations**: Enhancements to existing products, services, or processes that drive incremental growth.
- **Adjacent Innovations**: Expanding into new but related markets, technologies, or business models.
- **Transformational Innovations**: High-risk, high-reward initiatives that have the potential to redefine the industry.

By aligning resources and investment levels to these categories, companies can ensure that they are not over-investing in low-impact innovation or ignoring high-potential opportunities that could drive long-term transformation.

2. Creating Agile Knowledge-Sharing Networks

A company's ability to innovate is often limited by how well it facilitates knowledge-sharing across teams and business units. Too often, information is siloed, leading to inefficiencies, duplicated efforts, or missed opportunities. An innovation ecosystem must prioritize:

- **Cross-functional collaboration**: Encouraging teams from different disciplines (engineering, marketing, operations) to work together on new ideas.
- **Internal idea marketplaces**: Platforms where employees can submit, discuss, and refine new concepts before they reach executive decision-makers.
- **Learning loops and feedback cycles**: Regular sessions where teams present findings, share failures, and refine their approaches based on collective insights.

Companies like Unilever and P&G have successfully used open innovation platforms to leverage knowledge from both internal and external sources, allowing them to accelerate product development without overburdening internal R&D.

3. Leveraging External Partnerships and Open Innovation

Not all innovation needs to come from within. Leading companies recognize the value of partnering with startups, research institutions, and even competitors to drive new breakthroughs.

How external collaboration enhances innovation ecosystems:

- **Startup incubators and accelerators**: Corporations can invest in early-stage companies that align with their long-term vision, creating a pipeline for disruptive ideas.
- **Joint ventures and research collaborations**: Working with universities and research centers to explore cutting-edge technologies that would be too risky or expensive to develop in-house.

- **Customer-driven co-creation**: Engaging end-users in the innovation process through beta testing, feedback loops, and participatory design processes.

One example is BMW's Startup Garage, which integrates external innovators into its R&D processes, allowing the company to experiment with new automotive technologies without bearing the full cost of development.

4. Balancing Stability and Agility in Corporate Structure

An innovation ecosystem must be flexible enough to encourage experimentation and iteration while still ensuring financial discipline and accountability. Companies can achieve this by structuring their organizations to include:

- **Autonomous innovation teams**: Small, fast-moving groups that have the freedom to explore and test new ideas without traditional corporate constraints.
- **Flexible funding mechanisms**: Instead of requiring long approval cycles, providing discretionary innovation funds that teams can access to test ideas quickly.
- **Innovation governance**: A leadership group responsible for aligning new ideas with broader corporate objectives while ensuring that promising innovations receive necessary support.

A successful case study of this approach is Microsoft's evolution under Satya Nadella, where the company shifted from a rigid corporate hierarchy to a more fluid, collaborative structure that allowed cloud computing, AI, and open-source initiatives to flourish.

An innovation ecosystem is not a single entity but a network of interconnected processes, teams, and strategies that work together to maintain both growth and disruption. Companies that integrate structured innovation frameworks, encourage collaboration, and leverage external partnerships are far better positioned to adapt to changing markets while continuing to scale.

Leadership Strategies for Balancing Stability and Disruption

The success or failure of balancing growth with disruption ultimately depends on leadership. Without a leadership team that actively encourages, funds, and integrates innovation, even the best ideas will fail to gain traction. Effective leaders must navigate between two competing demands: protecting and optimizing the company's core business while fostering an environment where disruption is welcomed rather than resisted.

This requires a leadership mindset shift: from one that prioritizes control and risk reduction to one that embraces adaptability, calculated experimentation, and long-term strategic bets.

1. Leading with a Vision for Both Growth and Disruption

Leaders must communicate a compelling vision that includes both stability and innovation. Companies that struggle to balance these forces often fail because their leadership focuses too heavily on one side: either emphasizing operational efficiency at the expense of innovation or pursuing disruption without a sustainable growth plan.

A strong leadership strategy includes:

- **Clarity on the long-term vision**: Employees and stakeholders must understand how disruption fits into the company's broader growth plan.
- **Defining innovation objectives alongside financial goals**: Innovation cannot be an afterthought; it must be integrated into financial planning, operational goals, and performance metrics.
- **Empowering teams to take ownership of disruption**: Leaders must create an environment where employees feel confident in exploring bold ideas without waiting for top-down directives.

2. Structuring Leadership for Agility and Accountability

One of the biggest barriers to innovation is hierarchical decision-making. Traditional corporate structures often create bottlenecks where executives at the top control all strategic decisions. This slows down disruptive initiatives, as new ideas must pass through layers of approvals before being tested.

To combat this, successful companies implement distributed leadership models, where:

- **Decision-making authority is pushed to the front lines**: Employees closer to customers and market trends have the autonomy to make innovation-driven choices.
- **A balance between stability and risk-taking is built into leadership incentives**: Senior executives should be rewarded not just for efficiency improvements but also for their ability to foster and integrate new ideas.
- **Innovation leadership teams work in tandem with operational executives**: This ensures that disruptive

initiatives align with the company's broader financial and business objectives.

3. Aligning Culture and Incentives with Innovation Goals

A common mistake among large organizations is expecting innovation to flourish while maintaining a rigid corporate culture that punishes failure and rewards predictability. Leaders must actively shape a culture where innovation is seen as a necessary, ongoing process rather than an occasional initiative.

Key cultural and incentive shifts include:

- **Recognizing and rewarding intelligent risk-taking**: Employees should not fear failure when pursuing innovative projects. Instead, leaders should reward efforts that challenge the status quo, even if the end result is not an immediate success.

- **Establishing innovation-friendly compensation structures**: Traditional incentive models often prioritize cost-cutting and quarterly performance. Companies must introduce longer-term innovation bonuses, venture-based compensation, or equity stakes in new initiatives to align incentives with disruptive efforts.

- **Embedding innovation metrics into executive performance reviews**: Instead of measuring leaders solely on revenue and operational efficiency, companies should assess their success in fostering new business models, market expansion, and technology adoption.

4. Navigating Internal Resistance to Disruption

Even the most forward-thinking leaders will face internal resistance when pushing for disruptive change. Employees, middle managers, and even senior executives often resist innovation because they fear its impact on their current roles or profit centers.

To manage this resistance, leaders must:

- **Frame disruption as an opportunity, not a threat**: Instead of positioning innovation as a replacement for existing jobs or business units, leaders should highlight how it creates new opportunities for career growth and market expansion.
- **Lead by example**: Executives should actively participate in innovation initiatives, whether by sponsoring pilot projects, mentoring intrapreneurs, or taking calculated risks themselves.
- **Encourage open dialogue and collaboration**: Internal resistance often stems from a lack of understanding about why disruption is necessary. Leaders must foster transparent conversations that engage employees in shaping the future of the business.

Balancing growth with disruption requires more than structural adjustments; it demands a fundamental leadership transformation. The companies that succeed in this balance are led by executives who champion risk-taking, create organizational agility, and align incentives with long-term innovation goals.

As industries continue to evolve at an accelerating pace, leadership will be the defining factor in determining which companies survive and which become obsolete. In the next section, we explore how businesses can scale innovation efforts without losing the agility that makes disruption possible.

Scaling Disruptive Innovation Without Breaking the Business

While fostering disruption is essential for long-term survival, scaling it effectively is where many companies struggle. Disruptive ideas often start in isolated teams or experimental divisions, but without a clear roadmap for scaling, they either remain stuck in perpetual pilot mode or fail due to misalignment with the broader business.

Scaling disruptive innovation is particularly challenging because the structures and processes that ensure operational efficiency can be incompatible with high-risk, fast-moving innovation efforts. Companies that fail in this phase either overprotect disruptive ventures, preventing them from integrating with the core business, or rush them into the mainstream operation before they are fully mature, leading to failure.

To avoid these pitfalls, organizations must develop a structured yet flexible approach to scaling disruptive innovation, ensuring that breakthrough ideas can transition from experimental projects to fully integrated growth drivers.

1. Gradual Integration Through Phased Scaling

Companies often make the mistake of either keeping disruptive innovations too isolated or integrating them too quickly, leading to resistance from existing business units. Instead, a phased scaling approach allows innovation to mature while gradually aligning it with the organization's operational capabilities.

A successful phased scaling model includes:

- **Pilot Phase**: The innovation is tested in controlled environments or niche markets with limited risk exposure.
- **Incubation Phase**: The project receives increased funding and talent resources while being refined based on market feedback.
- **Expansion Phase**: The innovation scales into broader markets with cross-functional alignment and executive backing.
- **Full Integration or Spin-off**: The disruptive innovation is either fully absorbed into the core business or spun off as a separate entity if it does not align with existing structures.

Tesla exemplifies this model, gradually refining its electric vehicle technology in limited production runs before scaling to mass production while maintaining a degree of autonomy from traditional automotive manufacturing.

2. Creating Dedicated Pathways for Scaling Innovations

For disruptive ideas to scale successfully, companies must have a structured pathway that bridges the gap between experimentation and large-scale execution. This requires building dedicated scaling mechanisms, such as:

- **Innovation Transfer Teams**: Cross-functional groups responsible for adapting disruptive innovations to fit broader business processes without stifling their agility.
- **Corporate Venture Arms**: Investment teams that support internal startups and help scale them while keeping their entrepreneurial spirit intact.

- **Strategic Partnerships**: Collaborations with external organizations that can help scale innovations faster than internal capabilities allow.

A prime example is Google's approach to scaling innovations through Alphabet, which provides a flexible structure for experimental ventures while allowing successful projects to transition into Google's core business.

3. Aligning Financial Metrics with Long-Term Innovation Goals

One of the biggest barriers to scaling innovation is misaligned financial metrics. Traditional businesses are evaluated based on short-term profitability, whereas disruptive innovations often require years of investment before yielding significant returns.

To overcome this challenge, companies must adopt alternative financial models for disruptive ventures, including:

- **Long-Term Investment Horizons**: Evaluating success based on future market potential rather than immediate profitability.
- **Stage-Gated Funding Models**: Allocating capital in incremental phases, allowing high-potential projects to secure more funding as they meet key milestones.
- **Separate Financial Metrics for Innovation**: Measuring disruptive ventures based on market traction, learning outcomes, and ecosystem impact rather than traditional revenue and margin expectations.

Amazon's ability to reinvest profits from its core business into new ventures like AWS and Alexa demonstrates how financial discipline and innovation investment can coexist.

4. Managing Cultural and Organizational Resistance to Scaling

Even when an innovation proves successful in early trials, internal resistance can derail scaling efforts. Employees in the core business may view disruptive innovations as threats to their roles or existing revenue streams.

To address this challenge, companies should:

- **Proactively communicate the strategic rationale for scaling innovation**: Employees should understand how disruptive ventures complement the company's long-term vision rather than replace existing business units.
- **Incentivize collaboration between innovation teams and core operations**: Aligning compensation and career development incentives can encourage business units to support rather than resist scaling efforts.
- **Embed change agents within the organization**: Leaders who champion innovation can bridge the gap between disruptive initiatives and traditional business functions.

Scaling disruptive innovation without breaking the business requires a thoughtful blend of phased integration, structured scaling pathways, financial adaptability, and cultural alignment. Companies that succeed in this balance will not only drive sustained growth but also continuously reinvent themselves to stay ahead of industry shifts.

In the next chapter, we explore how companies can future-proof their innovation strategies, ensuring that disruption remains an ongoing process rather than a one-time initiative.

Conclusion: Achieving Sustainable Growth Through Scalable Innovation

Balancing growth with disruption is not a one-time challenge; it is a continuous effort that requires strategic discipline, cultural adaptability, and leadership commitment. Companies that master this balance become self-renewing organizations, capable of evolving with market shifts while maintaining the stability needed for long-term success.

To thrive in an era of rapid change, businesses must view innovation as an essential function, not an isolated department or occasional initiative. The organizations that successfully scale disruptive ideas without destabilizing their core operations will be the ones that dominate their industries, setting the pace for progress rather than reacting to it.

Key takeaways from this chapter:

- Scaling innovation requires structured yet flexible integration. Companies must ensure that breakthrough ideas transition smoothly from small-scale experiments to fully operational business units.
- Financial alignment is crucial. Companies must develop investment models that support disruptive innovation without compromising overall profitability.
- Culture and incentives must reinforce innovation. Without an organizational culture that embraces risk and continuous learning, even the best ideas will fail to gain traction.

As industries continue to evolve at an accelerating pace, the ability to balance stability and disruption will define the next generation of corporate leaders. The question is not whether companies should embrace innovation; it is how they can do so in a way that ensures longevity, scalability, and meaningful impact.

With the increasing pace of technological advancement, evolving consumer expectations, and global economic shifts, the very nature of corporate innovation is changing. The traditional models of research and development, incremental product improvements, and market-driven expansion are no longer sufficient for companies seeking to maintain a competitive edge.

In the next chapter, we will explore the future of corporate innovation: how emerging technologies, new business paradigms, and evolving leadership philosophies are reshaping how companies approach disruption. From artificial intelligence and blockchain to open innovation ecosystems and decentralized decision-making, the next frontier of innovation will require a radically different mindset. The companies that embrace these new models will shape the future of business, while those that resist will find themselves left behind.

CHAPTER 9

The Future Company, Designing Innovation Into the DNA

The Company That Never Waits

The future no longer sends advance notice. It doesn't arrive with press releases or research grants, it slips quietly into the edges of the market: a small start-up with a sharper idea, a new algorithm that rewrites the economics of an entire category, a shift in behavior invisible to anyone who isn't looking closely enough. The world now moves in real time, and the organizations that survive are those that move *with* it, not after it.

The company that never waits doesn't stand at the window watching the horizon, it *builds on it while it moves.* It knows that opportunity decays fast. Every week of hesitation erodes advantage, not because competitors are smarter, but because the feedback loop of learning has collapsed to near zero. To stay relevant is no longer a matter of having the best plan; it's about having the shortest distance between sensing and acting.

This company treats motion as intelligence. It learns while doing, adjusts while learning, and treats every cycle of iteration as a conversation with reality. Its currency is not forecasts but feedback. Its strength is not foresight but reflex. It recognizes that strategy can no longer be an annual ritual, it's a daily behavior. The question is no longer "What will the market look like next year?" but "What is the market teaching us this week?"

Inside the company that never waits, momentum is the new discipline. Speed isn't chaos, it's choreography. Each team moves with autonomy but aligns through shared intent. The center doesn't dictate direction; it defines meaning. Leadership becomes the designer of context, not the controller of activity. Everyone knows *why* they are moving, even if the *how* evolves every day.

There's an electric quality to the culture. Meetings feel shorter, but conversations are sharper. Decisions happen in days, not months, because people are trusted to decide. The operating rhythm feels alive, like a living network constantly adjusting its own flow to match the shape of reality. Planning and execution merge into a single continuous cycle of sensing, deciding, and adapting.

In such an environment, information travels at the speed of trust. The slowest part of the system is no longer the process, it's hesitation. So the company designs its nervous system to minimize hesitation: open data, shared dashboards, visible metrics. Everyone can see what's happening in real time. No one waits for permission to learn.

When something new emerges, a customer signal, a product insight, an unexpected failure, the organization doesn't convene a committee; it reacts. Not rashly, but responsively. Small experiments start immediately. Decisions are provisional, but progress is constant.

The future company does not fear incomplete information; it fears inertia. It knows that progress in uncertainty comes not from predicting, but from *approaching*. Every iteration gets it closer to the truth. It doesn't chase certainty; it manufactures it through learning.

And so, it's not driven by plans, but by *pulse*. It feels alive because it's always listening, always moving, always slightly out of balance, not because it's unstable, but because it's *growing*.

Waiting used to mean discipline. Now, it means surrender. The company that never waits doesn't rush blindly into the future; it simply refuses to be left behind by it.

From Hierarchies to Reflexes

If the industrial company was a machine, the future company is a nervous system. Machines obey; nervous systems sense. Machines execute instructions; nervous systems interpret stimuli and respond. This shift, from execution to interpretation, is the defining transformation of modern enterprise.

Hierarchies were built for a world that moved predictably. They optimized for control, consistency, and compliance. Their purpose was to ensure that what worked yesterday would work again tomorrow. But in an era when the ground shifts underfoot every quarter, the virtue of consistency becomes a liability. Control delays response. Consensus slows motion. The pyramid, once a symbol of strength, becomes a monument to latency.

The future company doesn't reject structure, it rewires it. It replaces the vertical chain of command with horizontal reflex arcs: networks of teams that can sense, decide, and act without waiting for orders from above. The organization starts to resemble an ecosystem more than an empire. The goal is no longer to maintain order, but to maintain flow.

At the core of this evolution is a simple premise: Decisions belong to proximity, not authority. Those closest to the signal, the customer, the problem, the data, have the mandate to act. Leadership shifts from directing to designing: creating the systems, principles, and guardrails that enable decentralized intelligence to function safely and coherently.

This doesn't mean chaos. It means context. The future company defines purpose so clearly that decisions can be made without constant supervision. When everyone understands the "why," the "what" and "how" can evolve freely. Alignment comes from meaning, not meetings. Coordination comes from transparency, not control.

In this model, information flows differently too. Instead of trickling upward through layers of translation, it circulates openly. Dashboards replace memos. Shared metrics replace management reports. Teams see the same data leadership sees, and act on it faster. The system learns as a whole.

What emerges is a reflexive organization:

- A customer insight surfaces in the morning; a prototype is built by evening.
- A field technician identifies a recurring issue; an update is deployed before headquarters convenes a task force.
- A new technology appears; the company tests it, not debates it.

This is how responsiveness replaces hierarchy, not by dismantling authority, but by redistributing it. The old question, "Who decides?" evolves into a new one: "Who senses first?"

The Architecture of Reflex

A reflexive organization operates on networks of trust and intent. Teams are autonomous but interdependent, connected through shared principles and real-time data. Feedback loops replace reporting lines. Every function becomes both sensor and actor, part of a continuous cycle of detection and adaptation.

The best analogy isn't corporate, it's biological.In the human body, the brain doesn't micromanage every movement. Reflexes occur locally, fast, precise, contextual. The brain provides purpose and interpretation, but the body moves before conscious thought catches up. This is how it survives. The future company functions the same way: *purpose at the center, reflex at the edge.*

When the structure works, the company feels less like a command center and more like a network of living intelligence. It listens faster than it plans. It acts faster than it explains. It learns faster than it fails.

This architecture demands trust, trust in people, in judgment, in the learning process itself. Without it, reflexes freeze. With it, they multiply.

In the end, hierarchy doesn't disappear; it evolves from control to coordination. Leadership remains essential, but its role changes: not to approve every move, but to design a system capable of moving without constant approval. The measure of leadership becomes how much speed it enables, not how much it governs.

The company that never waits cannot depend on a hierarchy that does. It needs a living structure, one that feels, learns, and reacts at the speed of its environment. It doesn't choose between order and agility. It designs *for both.* It's not a flatter company; it's a smarter one.

The next evolution is not about changing who leads, but how the organization itself thinks, from authority to awareness, from command to reflex.

Designing for Perpetual Beta

The companies that thrive in the future will not be the ones that perfect their systems, they'll be the ones that keep them unfinished.

To exist in perpetual beta is to treat every process, every product, and every assumption as a living prototype. It's to acknowledge that nothing is ever final, not because it's broken, but because it's surrounded by motion. The market evolves, technology accelerates, customer expectations rewrite themselves in real time. In such a world, stability is an illusion, and iteration is the only sustainable state.

Perpetual beta is not a slogan. It's a mindset built into the design of the organization.

It requires humility, the willingness to see every success as temporary, every process as transient, every strategy as conditional. It replaces the comfort of certainty with the discipline of renewal. The company becomes less a monument to what it has built and more a vessel for what it's becoming.

In traditional organizations, the assumption was that excellence comes from refinement, perfecting the model, eliminating variation, optimizing for predictability. But perfection in a changing world is a form of obsolescence. The longer something stays "finished," the less relevant it becomes.

The future company learns to live in iteration.

It treats launches not as endings, but as beginnings. A new product release is not a declaration of completion; it's an invitation to learn. Each version teaches the next. The same applies to teams, to strategies, to structures. Everything is open to revision, not because the company is uncertain, but because it is awake.

The Cycle of Renewal

Perpetual beta creates a culture of continuous calibration.

Instead of long planning horizons, there are rolling loops of observation, experimentation, and adjustment. The company moves like a flock, constantly sensing, slightly shifting, maintaining direction through collective awareness rather than central command.

This culture changes how time itself is experienced.

Meetings become checkpoints for learning, not ceremonies of compliance. Metrics are dynamic, updated in real time, emphasizing trajectories over targets. A plan is valuable only as long as it accelerates learning; once it slows it down, it's rewritten.

Employees feel this shift. They're not managed by stability but guided by purpose. They know that their work will evolve, and that evolution is not rework, but progress. The anxiety of change is replaced by the expectation of it.

This mindset builds resilience.

In a volatile world, companies that treat change as disruption are constantly recovering. Companies that treat it as respiration, as part of the rhythm of life, are constantly renewing. Their advantage isn't speed alone; it's durability through adaptability.

The irony of perpetual beta is that it produces more confidence, not less.

When teams know that they are designed to adapt, uncertainty loses its power. Risk becomes normalized. Learning becomes habitual. Failure becomes information, not identity.

From Perfection to Precision

Perfection was the goal of the industrial company, to create products and processes so refined they could be repeated indefinitely. But in a dynamic environment, repetition is regression. The goal now is precision in the moment, the ability to align perfectly with reality as it changes. Precision, unlike perfection, has a half-life. It must be renewed constantly.

Perpetual beta is how precision stays alive.

It doesn't mean abandoning quality; it means redefining it as responsiveness. It's the understanding that every great product, every great organization, is a conversation with time, and the future doesn't repeat its questions.

In practice, this means shorter cycles, smaller bets, and faster corrections. The company invests less in predicting what will happen and more in preparing to respond to whatever does. It measures readiness, not just performance. Its confidence doesn't come from control, but from competence, the earned ability to navigate flux without fear.

To design for perpetual beta is to commit to evolution as a way of life.

It's not a temporary mode of innovation; it's the permanent operating condition of relevance. The company stops asking, "When will we be ready?" and starts asking, "How can we keep becoming?"

The organization that learns to live this way stops chasing the future.

It becomes part of it.

Institutional Reflex vs. Institutional Memory

The future company doesn't rely on remembering; it relies on *responding*. Its strength lies not in how much it knows, but in how quickly it can learn again. Knowledge is no longer an archive, it's a current. The real advantage comes from how fast experience can be converted into action.

In this company, information doesn't move upward for validation, it moves outward for collaboration. Every team is both a sensor and an actor, part of a living network that listens, learns, and adjusts in real time. The structure feels less like an organization chart and more like a nervous system: distributed, responsive, and aware.

Institutional reflex doesn't replace memory; it *animates* it. The company still carries its experience, but in motion. Lessons aren't stored in static reports; they're embedded in processes, shared platforms, and living playbooks that evolve as they're used. The past isn't frozen into policy, it's woven into intuition.

The design of this system follows three guiding principles. First, transparency over transmission: knowledge isn't hidden behind layers of authority but shared freely across the network, so that insight anywhere becomes improvement everywhere. Second, context over control: decisions happen where the signal is clearest, not where the title is highest. The company trusts proximity, not hierarchy. Third, learning over labeling: success isn't measured by compliance with precedent, but by how quickly the organization becomes aware of what's next.

When a new signal appears, a customer behavior, a market anomaly, a novel technology, the company reacts instinctively. A team experiments, another interprets, and within hours, the learning spreads. The system self-corrects before the competition notices the drift. Reflex replaces reporting. Awareness becomes action.

Institutional memory, meanwhile, evolves into a living archive, constantly revised, continuously verified. The company's experience doesn't sit in documentation; it circulates as shared awareness. Every project updates the collective mind. What once would have been written down as a case study becomes a new reflex, integrated, automatic, alive.

This kind of organization remembers without being trapped by its history. It honors the principles that define it but refuses to enshrine the forms that once served them. It knows that procedures expire faster than purpose. It protects its DNA by letting its cells renew.

The outcome is rare: wisdom that moves at the speed of relevance. The company remains coherent but never static, grounded but never fixed. It is as aware as it is agile, capable of learning faster than its environment can surprise it.

The future company doesn't fear forgetting; it fears inertia. Because in a world defined by motion, only the organizations that *think in reflex* will stay alive long enough to remember why they exist.

The Operating Model of Adaptation

In the future company, adaptability is not an initiative, it's the operating system.

It's the invisible code running beneath every decision, project, and conversation. Where the old company optimized for efficiency, the adaptive company optimizes for *responsiveness*, the ability to sense, interpret, and act at the same rhythm as its environment.

Adaptation is not a reaction; it's a design choice. Every element of the company, structure, metrics, incentives, and communication, is arranged to maximize the speed and fidelity of learning. Strategy becomes less about prediction and more about preparedness. The company stops trying to forecast the future and instead builds the capacity to absorb it.

Inside such an organization, information flows like oxygen. Teams don't hoard data; they share it openly, knowing that awareness is what keeps the system alive. Feedback isn't a quarterly report, it's a constant pulse. Dashboards update in real time, linking every function through a common rhythm. Engineers see the same customer feedback that marketing sees. Operations sees the same demand signal that design does. Everyone interprets, acts, and adjusts in synchrony.

This coherence doesn't come from control; it comes from context. Leadership defines intent, the "why", and trusts the system to determine the "how." Strategy is expressed as direction, not instruction. The company replaces rules with principles, because principles scale better than policies. They allow variation without chaos, speed without fragmentation.

The result is an organization that behaves less like a machine and more like a living network. It pulses. It senses. It self-corrects. When one node detects a disruption, a new competitor, a shift in regulation, an emerging technology, the awareness spreads instantly. The company realigns without waiting for formal announcements or layers of approval. What used to take quarters now happens in days.

The adaptive model thrives on micro-decisions, small, rapid, reversible moves made close to the signal. Each of these decisions creates a ripple of learning, refining the company's overall direction through thousands of real-time calibrations. Progress emerges not from one grand plan, but from the cumulative intelligence of many fast experiments.

In this environment, learning replaces planning as the dominant rhythm. Plans still exist, but they are lighter, more flexible, frameworks for discovery rather than predictions of outcomes. The company thinks in hypotheses, not certainties. Every initiative begins with the question: *What must we learn to move forward?*

Measurement evolves, too. The future company tracks rate of learning as seriously as it once tracked rate of return. It measures how quickly an idea moves from conception to validation, how rapidly feedback translates into change, how fast a failure produces a new insight. The organization becomes a laboratory for velocity itself.

Incentives align accordingly. Success is defined by responsiveness, not compliance. Teams are rewarded for accelerating collective understanding, for making the company smarter, not just bigger. Recognition shifts from ownership to contribution, from protecting territory to expanding awareness.

The beauty of this model is that it scales through trust, not control. Leaders design the environment, then get out of its way. Their work is to maintain clarity of intent, remove friction, and keep the system focused on purpose. Adaptation becomes not a crisis response but a constant state of readiness, an institutional reflex honed by repetition.

The future company operates like a living algorithm: It senses the world, learns from every interaction, and evolves through feedback loops that never stop turning. Its edge isn't prediction; it's *perception*. Its advantage isn't speed for its own sake, but speed with awareness.

In a time when change is continuous, this is the only sustainable form of order, a system designed not to resist disruption, but to ride it.

The Augmented Organization

The next evolution of the adaptive company is not just speed, it's intelligence. As information multiplies and complexity deepens, organizations face a cognitive threshold: there is simply more to know than humans can process, and more change than they can track. Artificial intelligence emerges not as a replacement for people, but as the missing layer of perception, a force that extends awareness across dimensions no human team can see alone.

AI becomes the company's second nervous system. Where traditional reflexes operate on human sensing and interpretation, artificial intelligence adds scale, memory, and foresight. It observes everything: product telemetry, market signals, customer sentiment, environmental shifts. It connects patterns across silos that once operated blind to each other. Decisions once based on intuition alone now draw on a dynamic web of contextual intelligence.

In the augmented organization, humans and machines form a continuous loop of awareness. Data flows from the edges to the core and back again, collected by sensors, analyzed by algorithms, interpreted by humans, and refined into new questions. AI turns what used to be hindsight into foresight; it sees the faint signals that precede disruption and translates them into actionable possibilities before the rest of the market notices.

AI is not an oracle; it is an amplifier. It sharpens judgment by removing noise, freeing people to focus on what truly requires human discernment: purpose, meaning, ethics, and imagination. The organization becomes cognitively ambidextrous, machines handle scale and complexity, while humans navigate ambiguity and consequence.

This partnership changes the shape of leadership itself. Leaders no longer ask, *"What do we think?"* but *"What can we learn now that we couldn't see before?"* Decision-making shifts from authority to *augmented awareness*. Leaders become designers of questions, not just deciders of answers. Their work is to define intent clearly enough that the algorithms know what to optimize for, and what to leave untouched.

In this company, AI operates everywhere but commands nowhere. It recommends, simulates, predicts, and even prototypes, but final decisions remain human. The role of AI is not to dictate, but to illuminate; not to control, but to accelerate. Its power lies in its ability to compress time, collapsing the distance between sensing, understanding, and acting.

A marketing engine that once tested messages monthly now runs millions of micro-experiments in minutes. A design team uses generative models to produce hundreds of variations overnight, learning from each iteration. A logistics network reconfigures itself autonomously when weather or demand shifts. The adaptive organization learns continuously, even while it sleeps.

But this intelligence brings a new responsibility. Algorithms can calculate what is efficient, but not what is *right*. They can model outcomes, but not consequences. The company that never waits understands that ethics moves slower than technology, and that wisdom must evolve as quickly as capability. AI expands perception, but meaning still requires conscience.

The organizations that thrive will be those that pair machine speed with human depth. They will design governance as carefully as algorithms, ensuring that transparency, bias mitigation, and explainability are built into the system's DNA. Trust will become the new competitive advantage, not just in data accuracy, but in moral reliability.

The greatest gift of AI is not automation; it's amplification. It allows organizations to think at scale, to perceive patterns no human could, and to experiment at speeds once impossible. But its greatest limitation is also its lesson: it cannot decide what matters. That remains a human act.

The future company uses AI to anticipate the world, but depends on humans to interpret it. Together, they create a system where knowledge becomes reflex, foresight becomes culture, and adaptation becomes almost instinctive.

Artificial intelligence doesn't make the company less human; it makes it more conscious, aware of its choices, faster in its learning, and clearer about its purpose. It gives the enterprise a new kind of intelligence: one that listens as widely as it acts, one that connects insight with intention.

In the end, the augmented organization is not defined by its algorithms, but by how wisely it uses them. AI gives the company new eyes, but it is still the people who decide where to look.

The Human Trigger

For all its systems, sensors, and data flows, the future company still begins and ends with a person who decides to act. Adaptation may be engineered, but initiative is human. Every reflex in the organization, every signal interpreted, every change executed, traces back to someone who saw differently, who moved first, who refused to wait.

Technology amplifies this responsiveness, but it doesn't create it. Tools automate awareness, algorithms accelerate interpretation, yet the decision to trust the signal, to respond before it's obvious, remains an act of judgment. The company may be built on information, but it runs on courage.

In the adaptive enterprise, leadership becomes a distributed function, not a title. Everyone is expected to lead within their field of awareness, to connect their insights to the company's intent. The line between leadership and contribution fades; what matters is *response ownership*: the willingness to turn awareness into motion. The company becomes a choreography of small leadership moments, aligned by shared purpose.

The system thrives when its people understand that acting early is not recklessness, it's responsibility. In fast environments, waiting is the new negligence. To move with the future, individuals must reclaim a sense of authorship. The reflex to adapt starts not with technology or policy, but with mindset, a collective decision to stay alert, curious, and unfinished.

This is the paradox of modern organizations: the more automated they become, the more they depend on distinctly human qualities, intuition, empathy, creativity, and courage. Machines can surface patterns, but they can't decide what those patterns mean. Data can indicate direction, but it cannot define meaning. The company that never waits doesn't rely on code alone; it relies on conscience.

Every adaptive loop, every self-correcting system, requires a spark, a moment when someone feels something is shifting and chooses to respond. That choice, multiplied across thousands of people, becomes culture. Culture becomes reflex. Reflex becomes advantage.

In the end, the architecture of adaptation is a mirror. It reflects the intelligence and imagination of those who inhabit it. An organization can only move as fast as its people are willing to believe, decide, and act. The future company designs for this belief, it creates conditions where initiative feels safe, curiosity feels rewarded, and speed feels natural.

And that's the lesson of all the chapters before this one: innovation isn't a department, a lab, or a budget line. It's a behavior, one that begins in individuals and scales through trust. The company of the future doesn't wait because its people don't.

What happens next will depend on them. Because even the most adaptive system still needs a human trigger.

Conclusion

The future company is not an organization in the traditional sense; it's an evolving intelligence, part human, part algorithmic, constantly learning, constantly rewriting itself. It learns faster than it grows, and it grows because it learns. Its structure is porous, its rhythm continuous, its boundaries defined more by purpose than by geography or chart. It doesn't wait for certainty; it learns into it. Every process is provisional, every insight is iterative, every decision is an experiment that refines awareness.

In this company, artificial intelligence is woven into its nervous system. Data no longer waits to be analyzed; it thinks back. Algorithms translate complexity into clarity, amplifying the organization's perception. They sense shifts before they're visible, freeing people to focus on meaning, ethics, and imagination. Machines extend awareness; humans define direction. Together they form a continuous loop of cognition and conscience, a hybrid intelligence greater than either alone.

Information flows like breath, through humans and machines alike. Planning and execution coexist, feeding each other in real time. Teams act without permission because they are trusted with context. The culture rewards curiosity over caution, participation over perfection. Reflex becomes identity, and intelligence becomes collective.

Such an organization doesn't aspire merely to predict the future; it collaborates with it. It thrives not by eliminating volatility, but by metabolizing it, transforming uncertainty into understanding, and disruption into renewal. Its systems are alive, its people alert, its algorithms adaptive, its sense of purpose constant but never static.

This is the architecture of adaptation: a company designed to think, feel, and move at the speed of change, a company where technology amplifies awareness and humanity gives it meaning.

The future company may be built on code, data, and design, but its true evolution begins within the people who run it. The next transformation isn't structural, it's human. Building an adaptive organization requires leaders who can unlearn control and replace it with creation; who can sense before they instruct, and trust before they verify. The machinery of innovation is complete only when its operators think in possibility, not permission.

The following chapter explores that shift, from designing systems that adapt, to becoming leaders who embody adaptation itself. Because no algorithm can anticipate what only courage can decide.

The future company doesn't just use artificial intelligence, it becomes one.

CHAPTER 10

The Future Leader: From Control to Creation

The era of command is ending. For more than a century, leadership was defined by its ability to control, to plan, to predict, to ensure that the system behaved according to design. But in a world that no longer stays still, control has become the most fragile form of order. The leaders of the future do not stand above complexity trying to contain it; they move within it, shaping meaning as it unfolds.

The old leader sought certainty; the new one seeks sense. The first measured success by compliance, how faithfully others executed the plan. The second measures success by curiosity, how deeply others engage with the unknown. The role has evolved from commander to conductor, from planner to pattern-maker. Leadership is no longer about ensuring that things go right; it's about ensuring that people keep learning when they don't.

In the adaptive organization, power is not control, it's context. The leader's job is to design the environment in which reflexes thrive, where decisions can happen close to the signal without waiting for permission. Authority shifts from the person who knows the most to the one who enables the most learning. The best leaders today are architects of trust. They make clarity contagious.

This new kind of leadership begins with a different psychology. The future leader is comfortable with unfinishedness. They know that in complex systems, every decision is a prototype, a hypothesis to be tested, not a command to be enforced. They replace the illusion of certainty with the discipline of adaptation. Their confidence comes not from having the right answers, but from knowing how to frame better questions.

And where previous generations led through visibility and control, the new generation leads through presence and perception. They listen before they declare, learn before they decide, and design for possibility instead of compliance. They see culture as a medium, not a memo, something to be shaped, not announced.

The shift from control to creation is not a retreat from leadership; it's its renewal. Creation requires more courage than control. It demands the humility to let others lead, the patience to let systems self-organize, and the vision to guide by purpose rather than proximity. These leaders don't enforce direction, they compose it.

The great paradox of modern leadership is that the less you control, the more influence you have. When people act from understanding instead of obedience, they move faster, think deeper, and create more than any hierarchy could command. The future leader recognizes that influence flows not from authority but from alignment, the shared sense of why the work matters.

This new leadership is less about standing in front and more about standing among. It is relational, distributed, and deeply human, grounded in trust, powered by curiosity, and measured by how much better others become through your presence.

From Answers to Questions

Leadership once meant being the person who knew. The corner office was a monument to expertise, the place where experience accumulated into authority. But in a world that evolves faster than experience, knowing becomes brittle. Yesterday's expertise ages in months. The world no longer rewards those who have all the answers; it rewards those who know which questions to ask.

The future leader understands that curiosity is the new intelligence. In an adaptive company, questions are not signs of doubt, they are the engines of discovery. The leader's power lies not in ending debates, but in opening them in ways that move learning forward. They don't guard knowledge; they multiply it.

Artificial intelligence has changed what it means to be smart. Machines now store, retrieve, and process information with flawless precision and infinite memory. What they cannot do, what remains uniquely human, is to determine *which* problems matter, *why* they matter, and *what values* should shape the answer. The leader's mind becomes a filter for meaning, not merely a processor of facts.

In the future enterprise, human and machine intelligence form a partnership of opposites. AI accelerates pattern recognition, forecasting, and optimization. It can show what's probable, but not what's purposeful. It can simulate decisions, but not make moral ones. The leader's role is to bridge insight with intention, to turn prediction into progress.

This demands a new kind of literacy: question literacy, the ability to frame inquiry in ways that machines can calculate, and humans can interpret. When the organization faces complexity, the leader doesn't ask, "What should we do?" but "What do we need to learn?" When presented with data, they don't ask, "What does it say?" but "What might it be missing?" Their curiosity becomes strategic, a way to reveal blind spots before they become crises.

Questions are the operating code of the adaptive company. They spark experiments, reframe problems, and unlock imagination. Each one opens a new feedback loop between knowledge and action. In the best-led organizations, the number of good questions exceeds the number of premature answers. Curiosity is measurable, not in surveys, but in how fast new hypotheses replace old assumptions.

This form of leadership feels less like direction and more like dialogue. The leader no longer lectures; they listen, interpret, and synthesize. They create psychological safety for inquiry, signaling that asking is strength, not risk. In their presence, people stop defending what they know and start discovering what they don't.

When a company learns to lead with questions, it learns to evolve. Its leaders move from being the smartest people in the room to the most curious ones, not because they know more, but because they are willing to be surprised. And in a world driven by machine intelligence, the most valuable form of human intelligence will be precisely that: the courage to stay curious.

The Courage to Unlearn

In every era, leaders have been taught to master knowledge.

In this one, they must learn to release it.

The speed of change has made expertise perishable. Strategies, models, and management doctrines that once built empires now expire quietly within a fiscal quarter. What makes a leader valuable today is not the weight of what they know, but the lightness with which they can shed it.

Unlearning is harder than learning because it threatens identity.

For decades, control, confidence, and clarity were the currencies of authority. Leaders were trained to be the ones who knew. To admit uncertainty felt like weakness. To change one's mind felt like instability. But in a world where even the best models age in real time, rigidity is no longer strength, it's fragility disguised as conviction.

The future leader understands that relevance depends on renewal.

They treat their own thinking as a system to be continuously updated, questioning, refactoring, deleting old assumptions, rewriting mental code. They are their own perpetual beta. They know that experience, unexamined, becomes dogma; and that humility is not the absence of expertise, but the refusal to worship it.

Artificial intelligence accelerates this demand.

When machines can recall more, process faster, and predict better, the competitive edge for humans shifts from what they know to how they adapt. AI challenges leaders to see learning as an ongoing dialogue, a collaboration between evolving technology and evolving self. The question is no longer "What do I know that machines don't?" but "How can I evolve faster than the systems I build?"

This mindset requires courage, the courage to let go of the comfort of mastery.

Unlearning isn't erasing; it's updating. It's replacing the need to be right with the desire to stay relevant. It's the discipline of shedding habits that once made you successful but now make you slow.

The best leaders practice unlearning visibly.

They model it for their teams, changing course publicly, revising opinions without shame, rewarding those who surface inconvenient truths. In their cultures, the phrase "I was wrong" is not an apology;

it's an act of progress. They understand that every outdated belief they release creates space for a new idea to breathe.

Unlearning restores curiosity to experience.

It allows wisdom to remain flexible. It reminds leaders that knowledge is a tool, not a throne. The moment it becomes an identity, growth stops.

The organizations that thrive tomorrow will be led by those who are brave enough to be new again, who treat every success as provisional, every perspective as expandable, every failure as feedback.

To lead is no longer to know.

It's to keep becoming, faster than the world forgets what came before.

Leading with Presence and Perception

The faster the world moves, the more still the leader must become. In the noise of constant signals, data streams, dashboards, notifications, updates, presence has become the rarest form of clarity. The leader who can slow perception long enough to truly *see* is the one who guides meaning through motion.

Presence is not about visibility; it's about awareness. It's the ability to read the energy in a room, the mood of a team, the signal beneath the numbers. It's what allows a leader to sense disconnection before it turns into disengagement, to notice fatigue before it becomes failure. In a company where information travels faster than attention, presence is the last advantage that cannot be automated.

Artificial intelligence can analyze sentiment, but it cannot feel empathy. It can recognize patterns in behavior, but it cannot restore trust when it's broken. It can predict performance, but it cannot inspire purpose. That remains the work of human perception, of leaders attuned not just to metrics, but to meaning.

In adaptive organizations, emotional intelligence becomes structural intelligence. It is not a soft skill; it's the connective tissue that keeps reflexes coordinated. Without trust, information stalls. Without empathy, alignment fractures. Without psychological safety, curiosity disappears. The future leader designs for emotion as intentionally as for efficiency, knowing that fear and creativity cannot coexist in the same space.

Presence begins with listening, not the kind that waits to respond, but the kind that seeks to understand. The modern leader listens with their full attention, not just to people, but to the organization itself: its silences, its frictions, its pace. They listen to the *feel* of the system, the way a physician listens to a heartbeat, not to confirm health, but to detect rhythm.

Perception, then, becomes a form of strategy. The ability to sense the intangible, morale, motivation, momentum, becomes as valuable as financial acumen. The leader who perceives patterns in emotion can act with the same precision as one who reads patterns in data. They navigate culture with the same rigor they once reserved for markets.

This is leadership as awareness, quiet, intentional, deeply human. It doesn't announce itself through authority or title, but through resonance. Teams led by such people move faster not because they're told to, but because they feel seen, trusted, and safe to act. Presence creates coherence; perception sustains it.

In the age of AI, this becomes the human counterbalance, not a rejection of technology, but a re-centering of what machines cannot replicate: empathy, intuition, and trust. The future leader knows that systems think in data, but people move in emotion. Bridging the two is the art of leadership itself.

To lead with presence is to become the stabilizing force in motion, a still center in a spinning world. It's what allows an organization to act without fear, to experiment without paralysis, to move faster without losing its soul.

And it's how leadership, once defined by command, becomes defined by connection.

The Human Advantage

In a world increasingly defined by algorithms, the ultimate competitive advantage is humanity. When technology can think, calculate, and even create, what remains irreplaceable is the ability to care, to imagine, and to choose what *should* be done, not just what *can* be done. The future company may run on data, but it will be led by judgment.

Artificial intelligence gives leaders unprecedented clarity, but it cannot give them conscience. It can simulate creativity, but not curiosity. It can write symphonies, but not feel wonder. It can optimize decisions, but not define values. The work of leadership, deciding what matters and why, remains profoundly human.

As AI expands the organization's intelligence, it also expands its moral surface area. Every decision carries farther, touches more lives, and creates new ethical terrain. The leader's role, therefore, is not to outthink machines, but to out-human them, to infuse every act of intelligence with empathy and purpose.

The best leaders of the future will be moral designers as much as strategic ones.

They will architect trust into systems, embed fairness into algorithms, and ensure that speed never outruns integrity. They will understand that responsibility cannot be outsourced to automation, that ethics must evolve as quickly as capability.

This is what distinguishes leadership from management: the willingness to treat intelligence as a means, not an end. In the adaptive organization, decisions move fast, but meaning must move faster. Every new capability introduces a new question, not just "Can we?" but "Should we?" And it will fall to the leader to hold that tension between what is efficient and what is ethical.

The human advantage also lies in imagination, the ability to see what doesn't yet exist. AI can extrapolate from the past; humans can dream beyond it. The leader's imagination becomes a force multiplier, projecting visions that data alone could never conceive. It is imagination that transforms information into innovation, and emotion that turns innovation into movement.

The future leader's empathy, intuition, and creativity are not "soft" traits; they are strategic assets. Empathy aligns teams faster than any process. Intuition detects shifts before analytics confirm them. Creativity reframes problems that data alone cannot solve. These qualities transform the organization from intelligent to aware, from capable to conscious.

In a machine-driven world, leadership becomes the practice of staying human at scale. It's about maintaining moral gravity when technology tempts us toward weightlessness. It's about ensuring that intelligence, human or artificial, always serves life, not the other way around.

Because as powerful as machines become, the most valuable algorithm will remain the human mind guided by the human heart.

Legacy as Renewal

Every generation of leaders inherits not just an organization, but a worldview. The industrial age taught us to equate legacy with endurance, to build things that last, to leave behind monuments of structure and control. But in the age of perpetual change, longevity is no longer the measure of greatness. Relevance is. The legacy of the future leader is not what they preserve, but what they *renew.*

In adaptive organizations, permanence is replaced by continuity of learning. What endures is not a process or a hierarchy, but a pattern, a culture of curiosity, a rhythm of reinvention. The leader's true work is to design systems that outgrow them, to make evolution self-sustaining. Leadership success is no longer measured by how indispensable you become, but by how unnecessary you make yourself.

Artificial intelligence intensifies this redefinition. In a company that learns autonomously, the leader's imprint is not carved in stone; it's encoded in behavior, in the algorithms of culture, the ethics embedded in data, the values woven into decision systems. The question shifts from *"What did I build?"* to *"What did I teach the organization to become?"*

Legacy becomes a living thing, not a statue to be admired, but a signal that continues to evolve. The future leader's contribution is not a fixed vision, but a capacity for renewal, a cultural DNA that ensures the company remains open to the next transformation. They leave behind not stability, but motion; not instructions, but intent.

This form of leadership requires profound humility. To design for renewal is to accept that your greatest work will be rewritten, that your systems will be modified by others you may never meet. It's to find satisfaction not in control, but in continuity, in watching your ideas adapt long after you're gone.

Great leaders of the past wanted their organizations to remember them. Great leaders of the future will want their organizations to keep learning from them. Their true legacy will not be admiration, but acceleration, the ability to keep moving forward without losing meaning.

Because in a world defined by constant reinvention, legacy is not about leaving something behind. It's about leaving something alive.

Conclusion

Leadership, like innovation, is no longer a destination. It's a practice of renewal. a continuous act of becoming. The future company does not wait, and the future leader does not finish. Both exist in motion, learning their way forward through awareness, curiosity, and courage.

The greatest shift of this century is not technological, it's psychological. Artificial intelligence will change how we work, but leadership will determine why we work. Machines may master cognition, but meaning remains a human craft. The challenge for every leader is to guide intelligence, human and artificial, toward purpose, empathy, and creation.

Control once defined leadership; now it limits it. The future leader creates space, not certainty, conditions where others can experiment, learn, and grow. Influence flows not from authority, but from alignment. Power is measured not in how many decisions one makes, but in how much potential one unlocks.

The mark of great leadership in the age of AI will not be perfect foresight, but *moral imagination*, the ability to imagine better futures, design systems that enable them, and trust people enough to build them together.

And when that happens, leadership becomes less about command and more about consciousness, a state of shared awareness between people and technology, guided by values deeper than efficiency and ambitions larger than profit.

The leaders of tomorrow will be remembered not for how much they controlled, but for how boldly they created, and for how courageously they allowed others to do the same.

Because in the end, leadership is not about being followed. It's about leaving behind the conditions for progress, a culture capable of learning, adapting, and imagining long after you are gone.

That is the legacy of creation. That is the future of leadership.

Conclusion: The Future Belongs to the Bold

Every enduring company begins with an act of defiance. Someone, somewhere, once refused to accept that the way things are is the way they must remain. That defiance, not comfort, not process, not consensus, is what built every industry that matters. Innovation is never born from permission; it begins as rebellion, as a refusal to wait.

That spark is what turns a handful of people in a garage, a lab, or a dorm room into the architects of new markets. It's what transforms a fragile idea into a force. And yet, as history reminds us, the same forces that make a company strong can quietly make it slow. Growth brings scale, and scale brings gravity. Over time, the very structures built to preserve success begin to suffocate it.

This is the Growth–Innovation Paradox: the tragedy of success turning into safety. The startup that once chased possibility begins chasing predictability. Risk becomes something to minimize, not master. The company that once lived in motion begins to live in memory.

Kodak invented digital photography and buried it. Nokia owned mobile phones and dismissed the touchscreen. Blockbuster watched streaming rise and waited for proof. None of them failed because they were blind; they failed because they stopped believing they could be wrong. The danger wasn't ignorance, it was certainty.

Breaking the Cycle

But decline is not destiny. Some companies have broken this pattern, not by accident, but by design. Microsoft found renewal in humility, reinventing itself around learning and cloud innovation. Amazon institutionalized curiosity, treating experimentation as a business model. Tesla turned speed itself into a competitive advantage, refusing to let scale dull its sense of danger.

These companies prove that it's possible to grow without calcifying, to scale without slowing. They have designed for motion, building systems that learn faster than markets change. They've replaced rigid layers with feedback loops, bureaucracy with bandwidth, permission with accountability.

They show that innovation at scale isn't about size; it's about posture. It's about staying slightly off-balance, always stretching toward what's next.

The Choice Every Business Must Make

Every company, no matter how dominant, will face the same moment of reckoning. The market shifts. The customer evolves. Technology rewrites the rules. And suddenly, yesterday's best practices start to feel like handcuffs.

When that moment comes, leaders have only two choices:

- **Adapt,** challenge their own success, rewrite their own rules, and bet on new ideas while the old ones still work.
- **Or cling**, defend what is familiar, rationalize delay, and wait for clarity that never arrives.

History is merciless to those who choose the second path. Companies don't die from lack of intelligence; they die from lack of nerve.

The Age of Acceleration

The urgency has never been greater. The cycle of disruption that once took decades now unfolds in months. Artificial intelligence, automation, and global competition have collapsed the time between idea and obsolescence, forcing every organization to think in reflex and learn in real time.

The advantage no longer belongs to the largest or even the smartest, but to the fastest learners, those who build systems that evolve as quickly as the world around them.

But the same technologies that threaten incumbents also offer their redemption. AI can become the company's peripheral vision, turning information into instinct, pattern into perception, and data into direction. Automation can free human creativity instead of replacing it. Data can turn hindsight into foresight, if leaders are willing to listen to it, and act.

The question is not whether disruption will happen, but whether it will come from you or to you.

The Next Generation

A new generation of leaders is already rewriting the rules. They are digital natives fluent in uncertainty, allergic to hierarchy, and impatient for progress. They don't ask for permission; they ask for clarity. They expect transparency, autonomy, and purpose, and they will give their full talent only to companies that embody those things.

For them, innovation isn't a slogan on a wall; it's a way of working, a moral choice. They understand that agility isn't chaos, it's integrity in motion. That building fast is not reckless if you learn faster. That the measure of a company's greatness isn't how long it has dominated, but how well it can begin again.

In these organizations, humans and algorithms learn together, machine speed meets human purpose, and progress becomes shared consciousness.

The companies that learn to breathe this air, open, fast, curious, morally awake, will not just attract the best minds; they will compound them. Because talent, like innovation, thrives where the system breathes.

Designing for Motion

Innovation is not a department. It is an operating temperature. You don't raise it with slogans or offsites; you raise it with design, decision rights at the edge, guardrails instead of gates, small bets with short half-lives, feedback at machine speed, and a culture that learns as easily as it executes.

To rebuild an organization's pulse is to make curiosity safe again, to give people the freedom to ask *"What if?"* and the tools to find out.

The Future That Breathes

Every company eventually faces the same question: Will we protect what we've built, or will we build what protects us?

The companies that endure, truly endure, are those that never forget what it felt like to be small: restless, experimental, unsatisfied.

They remember that progress doesn't come from certainty, but from movement. They design not for permanence, but for renewal.

Innovation, in the end, is not something you achieve. It's something you protect, from process, from fear, from the gravity of your own success.

Because long after the charts fade, long after the markets shift, what remains is motion, the continuous act of becoming.

The future does not belong to the biggest. It belongs to the bold, to those who keep moving, keep questioning, and keep building what doesn't exist yet.

And if you're reading this at the height of your company's success, remember this: success is not a finish line; it's a starting point.

The next chapter of your company's story is unwritten. Pick up the pen, and remember, the ink is motion.

Afterword: The Horizon Never Waits

The horizon is not a destination. It is a mirror, reflecting how far we've come and how much further we can still imagine. Every time we reach it, it moves. Not to mock our progress, but to remind us that motion is the point.

Innovation, like leadership, is never finished. It is the continuous act of seeing differently, of daring to build what others only discuss. The companies that survive the longest are not those that master change, but those that fall in love with becoming.

Artificial intelligence will accelerate this evolution, reshaping the edge of what's possible every day. But technology alone is not the future, *we* are. Machines may expand our sightlines, but it is courage that determines what we look for. They can generate a thousand paths forward, but only conscience can choose which one is worth walking.

The story of progress has always been a human one. It is written not by algorithms or systems, but by individuals willing to question what came before, to move, to imagine, to create. The future company is not an abstraction; it is built every day by those who act before certainty, who learn before proof, who trust motion over memory.

And so, as you close this book, remember: the horizon will never wait. Every idea, every invention, every generation of builders faces the same choice, to watch the future unfold or to help shape it.

The ones who shape it do not ask for permission. They begin.

Author's Note

Thank you for reading.

When I began writing *Trailblazing Products*, my goal was to help innovators and entrepreneurs bring bold ideas to life. This book continues that journey, from building disruptive products to building organizations that can keep disrupting themselves.

Both books were written with the same conviction: that progress is a choice. We can choose motion over maintenance, learning over legacy, creation over control. Whether you are leading a global company or starting something small in a garage, the same truth applies, the future favors those who keep moving.

If this book leaves you with only one thought, let it be this: innovation is not what we do; it's how we live. It is the daily discipline of curiosity, courage, and renewal. It is what keeps both companies and people alive.

Thank you for walking this path with me, for thinking, questioning, and imagining what might come next. May your work continue to breathe, evolve, and lead the way toward a future that never waits.

Souheil Benzerrouk

REFERENCES

Agazu, G. B., Sifer, A., & Wondifraw, M. A. (2025). Transformational leadership and firm performance: a systematic literature review. *Journal of Innovation and Entrepreneurship,* *14*(1), 29. https://www.researchgate.net/publication/389647837_Transformational_leadership_and_firm_performance_a_systematic_literature_review

Benzerrouk, S. (2025). *Too Big to Innovate: How Growth Stifles Disruption in Large Corporations.*

Benzaghta, A. M., Kourdi, H. O., El-Bassiouny, N. M., & Kourdi, M. O. (2022). Innovation management case study. *ResearchGate.* Retrieved from https://www.researchgate.net/publication/364403068_Innovation_Management_Case_Study

Bhatnagar, R., & Das, S. (2025). The concept of red tape and efficiency among corporate and government manager: Analysis on the effects to their management performances. *ResearchGate.* Retrieved from https://www.researchgate.net/publication/387666082_The_concept_of_red_tape_and_efficiency_among_corporate_and_government_manager_Analysis_on_the_effects_to_their_management_performances

Borja, A., & Martinez, P. (2022). Innovation and firm performance: The moderating and mediating roles of firm size and small and medium enterprise finance. *MDPI, 13*(5), 97. https://www.mdpi.com/1911-8074/13/5/97

Britto, R. (2022). Managing and executing innovation effectively in large-scale distributed organisations: A case study. *DiVA portal*. Retrieved from https://www.diva-portal.org/smash/get/diva2:1678926/FULLTEXT01.pdf

Hämäläinen, H., & Kaasinen, J. (2022). Rethinking the effect of risk aversion on the benefits of service innovations in public administration agencies. *ResearchGate*. Retrieved from https://www.researchgate.net/publication/315708496_Rethinking_the_effect_of_risk_aversion_on_the_benefits_of_service_innovations_in_public_administration_agencies

Heard, A., Kerxhalli-Kleinfield, D., & Holmes, A. (2022). *Management of innovation in organizations and the innovation imperative: Strategies and initiatives*. ResearchGate. Retrieved from https://www.researchgate.net/publication/364612794_Management_of_Innovation_in_Organizations_and_the_Innovation_Imperative_Strategies_and_Initiatives

Hendrastuti, H., & Harahap, D. T. (2024). Agency theory: Review of the theory and current research. *ResearchGate*. Retrieved from https://www.researchgate.net/publication/382295479_Agency_theory_Review_of_the_theory_and_current_research

Le Merle, M. C. (2023). *Corporate innovation in the fifth era: Lessons from Alphabet/Google, Amazon, Apple, Facebook, and Microsoft*. Scribd. Retrieved from https://www.scribd.com/document/19062386/Case-Studies-on-Managing-Innovation-Vol-I

López-Gómez, P. M., & Garcia-Fortea, D. (2022). Risk aversion, innovation and performance in family firms. *ResearchGate*. Retrieved from https://www.researchgate.net/publication/316865064_Risk_aversion_innovation_and_performance_in_family_firms

Nabi, M. S., & Khan, A. (2024, October 8). How Risk-Aversion Blocks Innovation. *Game-Changer*. Retrieved from https://www.game-changer.net/2024/10/08/how-risk-aversion-blocks-innovation/

OECD. (2024). *Investment Report 2024/2025: Innovation, integration and simplification in Europe*. EIB. Retrieved from https://www.eib.org/attachments/lucalli/20240354_investment_report_2024_en.pdf

Papadopoulos, P., & Dimopoulos, G. (2025). The relationship between innovation and risk taking: The role of firm performance. *MDPI, 11*(8), 144. https://www.mdpi.com/2227-9091/11/8/144

Rodrigues, R. G., Costa, J. C., & D'Este, P. (2025). Does bureaucracy demotivate public servants? An assessment of psychological mechanisms and the moderating role of age. *Taylor & Francis Online*. Retrieved from https://www.tandfonline.com/doi/full/10.1080/14719037.2025.2504723

Sarfraz, M. (2024). The impact of corporate governance, internal control and corporate reputation on employee engagement: a moderating role of leadership style. *Taylor & Francis Online*. Retrieved from https://www.tandfonline.com/doi/full/10.1080/23311975.2023.2296698

Schoenmaker, D., & Schot, J. (2022). *The entrepreneurial state: A European perspective*. Cambridge University Press. Retrieved from https://www.cambridge.org/core/elements/diversification-in-the-world-of-data-and-ai/DF96B29BB259357F9152D480EA83411B

Schumacher, S., & Schlaak, K. (2021). The relationship between firm size and innovation performance: A meta-analysis. *Journal of Business Economics, 91*(3), 457–481. https://link.springer.com/article/10.1007/s11573-021-01046-5

Stojanova, N. (2025). Challenges and opportunities for SMEs in supply chain digital transformation. *Journal of Advanced Business Research, 11*(1), 1–15. https://journals.scholarpublishing.org/index.php/ABR/article/download/18667/10809/26742

Taneja, V., & Singh, V. (2023). Artificial intelligence adoption in SMEs: Survey based on TOE–DOI framework, primary methodology and challenges. *Applied Sciences, 15*(12), 6465. https://www.mdpi.com/2076-3417/15/12/6465

Vasileiadou, E., & Nijkamp, P. (2020). Digital transformation and innovation: The influence of digital technologies on turnover from innovation activities and types of innovation. *MDPI, 12*(9), 359. https://www.mdpi.com/2079-8954/12/9/359

Weking, J., & Klein, D. (2023). Business model innovation through digital entrepreneurship. *Semantic Scholar*. Retrieved from https://pdfs.semanticscholar.org/909d/00a30035807a783f736b2cfd5aa89bf28b5f.pdf

World Economic Forum. (2025). *The Global Risks Report 2025*. Retrieved from https://reports.weforum.org/docs/WEF_Global_Risks_Report_2025.pdf

.

www.ingramcontent.com/pod-product-compliance
Lightning Source LLC
Chambersburg PA
CBHW060544200326
41521CB00007B/473